Brassey's *History of Uniforms*

Current titles

American Civil War: Confederate Army
American Civil War: Union Army
Napoleonic Wars: Wellington's Army
Napoleonic Wars: Napoleon's Army

Forthcoming titles

Mexican-American War 1846-48
English Civil War

Brassey's *History of Uniforms*

Napoleonic Wars
Napoleon's Army

By René Chartrand

Colour plates by Christa Hook

Series editor Tim Newark

To my sons

First English Edition 1996

UK editorial offices: Brassey's Ltd, 33 John Street, London
WC1N 2AT
UK Orders: Marston Book Services, PO Box 269, Abingdon,
OX14 4SD

North American Orders: Brassey's Inc,
PO Box 960, Herndon, VA 22070, USA

René Chartrand has asserted his moral right to be identified
as the author of this work.

Library of Congress Cataloging in Publication Data available
British Library Cataloguing in Publication Data
A catalogue record for this book is available from the British
Library

ISBN 1 85753 183 3 Hardcover

Typeset by Images Book
Production Ltd.

Printed in Great Britain by BPC Wheatons Ltd, Exeter

Contents

Introduction

The genesis of the uniforms worn by the French Army during the Napoleonic period owed much to the last major dress regulations of Louis XVI's royal army promulgated in 1786. While the colour of the infantry's coats changed from white to blue during the French Revolution, many details, and especially the cut of the coats, remained largely the same until the Imperial regulations decreed in 1812. The standing collars did get higher during the 1790s and cuff flaps were added but, by and large, lapels remained the same, each with its seven small buttons, and coat tails forming turnbacks remained long.

An alternative to the line infantry's long-tailed coats with squared and cut-away lapels, and, until 1807, bicorn hats, were the light infantry and chasseur units who wore short-tailed coatees with pointed lapels. They were already sporting shakos in the late 1790s, and long, tight trousers and short gaiters. All this supposedly made them more 'light' and nimble.

The French cavalry, and especially the light cavalry, saw an explosion of varied units in the early 1790s created more or less spontaneously and wearing just about every colour in the rainbow. Often raised among the wealthier classes of society, these units designed uniforms unhindered by any regulations. However, they were rationalized thanks to the genius for organization that the Minister of War, Lazare Carnot, possessed during this turbulent period. All sorts of hussars 'of Liberty' of 'Death' and so on were grouped into new regular units of Chasseurs à cheval and hussars and, after a time, adopted more 'standard' uniforms although the reader will doubt that any standardization occurred after seeing our chapter devoted to the light cavalry!

The heavy cavalry and dragoons saw relatively few changes during the 1790s. The 'Cavalerie' regiments too were often in rags, lacking equipment and their uniform did not radically change until converted into cuirassier regiments from 1803-1804. As for dragoons, their general appearance changed little from the 1780s

until 1812 when, like the infantry, they finally gave up the long-tailed coat for the short-tailed coatee.

Artillery, engineers and other specialist troops had few changes in dress during the Revolutionary period. National Guard or volunteer gunners only used a red collar on the standard artillery uniform instead of the blue piped red collar of the regulars which eventually remained the standard. Engineers too continued to use the same uniform. The creation of horse artillery regiments, however, brought the prevailing hussar fashion to that corps but in the more sober artillery colours of blue trimmed with red. Gunners everywhere are traditionally more conservative dressers than hussars.

At the head of this colourful parade was probably the most splendid and fashionable general staff in modern history. The flamboyant fashions of French revolutionary generals, something of an explosion of gold embroidery, lace, plumes, silk sashes and so on, competed strongly with the dandy 'incroyables' and 'merveilleuses' to be seen in the streets of Paris. Some order was attempted during the Consular and Imperial periods which did bring in more gracious dress but, by and large, to see Napoleon's marshals and generals was to see the heights of military fashion for general officers. The impression was such that most nations emulated these uniforms for a century to come.

In another sense, uniforms and uniformity of dress came to something of a peak during Napoleon's rule. With the advent of conscription from 1792, far more Frenchmen than ever before found themselves in uniform to do their military service. Thus was the concept of a national uniform born, forging new links between the country's army and its population at large. The wearing of military-style uniforms spread to occupations which were not essentially military such as customs, train drivers and many other types of civilian services. Like military uniform, the civilian uniforms gave a sense of order and efficiency to the public.

Hussar, c. 1800. Print after C. Vernet. J. Ostiguy, Ottawa.

Hues of colours

Among subjects of confusion, that of the exact colour
hues of uniforms ranks high. During the Revolutionary and Napoleonic period, many chemicals or
chemical effects were not understood with scientific
precision in a semi-industrial manufacturing context.
Thus, while there were general rules and dyestuffs
available, the dyeing of vast quantities of material
could vary according to the artisan's talents, the
ingredients used and the technical possibilities of the
equipment. Therefore, absolute uniformity in hue,
even on the same bolt of cloth was impossible.

Generally speaking, the colour blue was a very dark
blue generally known as 'Imperial blue'. The colour
green was also a very dark 'Imperial green'. Red
covered quite a lot of related hues such as 'garance',
usually given as a bright red, and scarlet which was
also a bright red, but of richer quality. But red could
also be somewhat darker pink with a touch of violet to
be 'amaranth'. In Britain and the United States,
crimson was a sombre dark red but in France, crimson
was brighter with a hard to define pinkish-violet hue,
even on surviving uniforms. On the other hand, 'puce'
was a dark crimson. A common colour for lace and

**Grenadier private of a line infantry half-brigade, 1793. This
soldier wears the new blue 'national' uniform with red
epaulettes and a hanger denoting his grenadier's status. The
crested cap was a remnant of the 1791 dress regulations.**
German print after Seele.

braid was 'aurore' which we have consistently
translated as orange since it was made with two parts
yellow mixed with one part red. Yellow was often
termed 'jonquille' to indicate a fairly bright yellow.
'Gris-de-fer' (literally: steel-grey) was a lightish blue-
grey. But many light blue-grey uniforms were actually

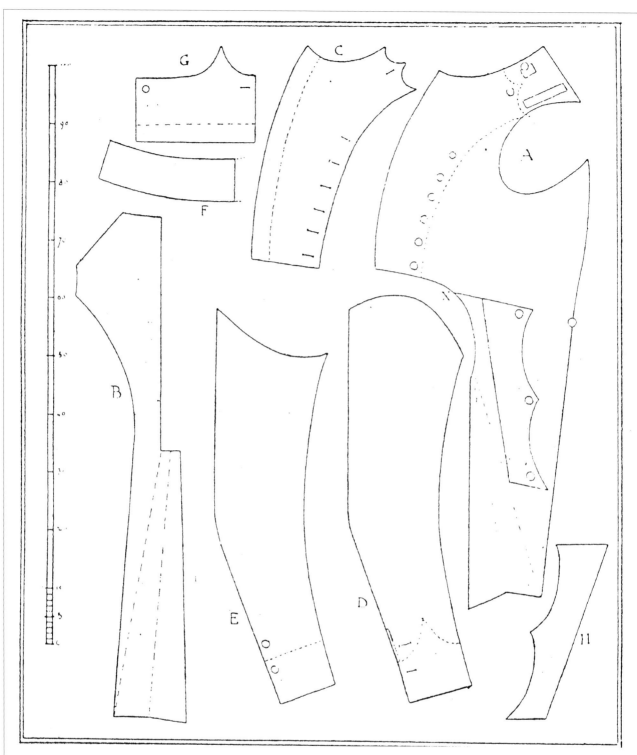

Pattern of an officer's coat, 16th Light Infantry Regiment, 1812 Regulations. A: front, B: back, C: lapel with its fold, D: top of sleeve, E: under sleeve, F: collar, G: cuff with its fold, H: pocket flap. Costumes et uniformes, 1912.

sky blue.

Last but not least, conditions in the field could have dramatic effects on uniforms colours and uniformity. Lieutenant Piéron of the 32nd Regiment of Line Infantry in southern Spain wrote in 1810: 'The replacement [clothing] for the troops occurs one or two years late. Our men are bare-footed, we cannot give them shoes. Imagine their dress! Everything sent from France, men, horses, supplies, is consumed [or diverted] on the way. Convoys take up to a year to reach us... A bad quality hat is worth 150 francs. Each man thus becomes in turn a tailor and a shoemaker; the most skilled cut, the others stitch. Pantaloons of brown cloth are much in wear by us, made with cloth found in convents; it is very much in fashion in the southern army...'

Hair styles
Queues and powdered hair were the regulation style at

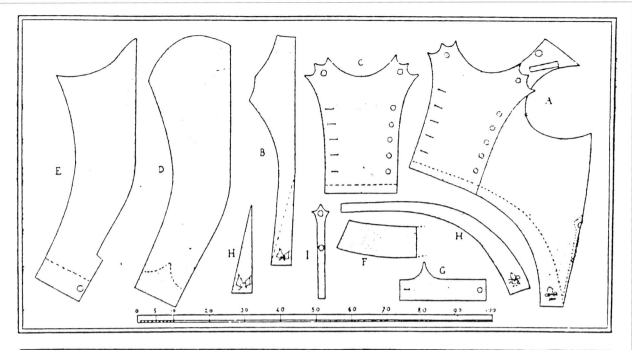

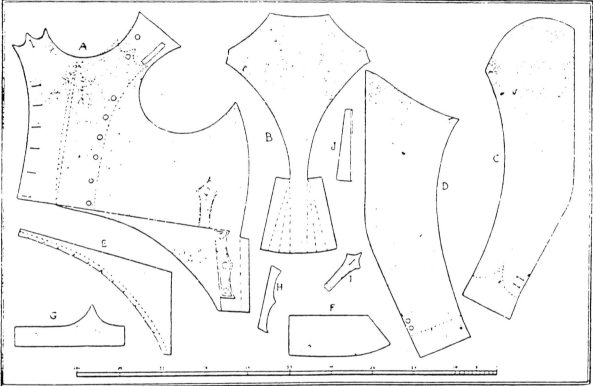

Pattern of an officer's coatee, 1st 'Chevau-Légers Lanciers' Regiment, 1814. A: front, B: back, C: double plastron, D: top of sleeve, E: under sleeve, F: half of collar, G: cuff, H: 'Soubise' type pocket flap. The lilies on the turnback were put on after Napoleon's abdication. Costumes et uniformes, 1913.

Pattern of a trooper's kurta, 2nd Lancers of the Imperial Guard, 1810-1815. A: front, B: back, C: top of sleeve, D: under sleeve, E: turnback, F: half of collar, G: cuff, H: pocket flap, I: belt loop, J: piped piece in the skirt. Costumes et uniformes, 1912.

the time of the Revolution. But at Boulogne in late 1803, Napoleon ordered the army to cut its queues, quit the messy powder and adopt the Neo-Roman 'Titus' style of short hair of natural colour. 'Many grumbled but all eventually submitted' says Constant, who meant all line troops. However, a few

infantrymen still had them five years later. 'The 36th of the line,' wrote Marshal Castellane in Spain during November 1808, '[was a] regiment of the small number [of units] in the infantry whose soldiers still wore the queue...' Hussars and Chasseurs à cheval were also ordered to adopt the new style, some regiments being most reluctant (see chapter 5). The

Old Guard units were allowed to keep their queues and powder.

Moustaches were the prerogative of grenadiers and hussars. Otherwise, all were clean-shaven (with sideburn) except for sappers who were the only men in the army allowed to wear beards.

Glossary

Bicorn hat ('Chapeau bicorne'): essentially a wide-brimmed hat folded to form two points.

Breeches ('Culottes'): fairly tight nether wear ending below the knee with a garter and side opening fastened by several small buttons. Worn by nearly all military and civilians on dress occasions. Hussar (or Hungarian) style breeches were tighter and went down lower.

Coat ('Habit'): the basic coat worn by most foot troops until 1812. It had long tails. The collar was standing. The cuffs were usually round with a cuff flap bearing three small buttons. The lapels each had seven small buttons and hooked at the top but flared away coming down. The bottom of the lapel was usually square but could also end in a point just below the waist, usually for light troops. The tails had at the top three-pointed pocket flaps, usually set horizontally but sometimes vertically.

Coatee ('Habit-veste'): essentially the same as the coat but with short tails. Before 1812, the coatee front would usually be flared. From 1812, the coatee had square lapels which hooked down to the waist completely hiding the waistcoat.

Epaulettes ('épaulettes'): in this book, epaulettes refer to a shoulder strap with fringes. Usually worn by elite troops in coloured wool and officers in gold or silver lace with bullion or strand fringes.

Forage cap ('Bonnet de Police' and, from 1812, 'Pokalem'): the 'Bonnet de Police' was a cap with a long crown that ended in a point with a tassel at the end and had a wide turnup. The crown was often folded in two and tucked in the turnup. The crown's seams and the turnup were edged with piping. The turnup also had a lace edging and, often, a badge or a numeral in front. This type of forage cap was rolled and fastened under the cartridge box flap, the tassel hanging bellow. The 'Pokalen' forage cap introduced in 1812 was a cap with a flat round crown and a wide headband, piped in the facing colour. However, many preferred the older type and continued to wear it.

Gaiters ('Guêtres'): protective leg wear of wool or linen with instep and closed at each side with many small buttons. Went above the knee until 1812 then below but the Old Guard infantry continued wearing the old style. On campaign, cut down or plain short gaiters were often worn. Light infantry had short gaiters which came at about mid-calf, usually edged and sometimes with tassel at top front.

Knapsack ('Sac à dos'): Made of cow-hide with hair outside, the top flap fastened by three buckles and straps, carried by straps around each shoulder. The greatcoat could be rolled, and sometimes put in a linen bag, and carried on top of the knapsack held by two and later three straps. Napoleon felt that, since soldiers packed all their worldly belongings in their knapsacks, they should not leave them in the field before a battle and lose them, as he had seen the Russian do at Austerlitz, so he insisted that 'the soldier should wear his knapsacks at all times'. Thus, the French Napoleonic army went into battle wearing knapsacks.

Kurta: Polish-style coatee worn especially by lancers. It featured piping on the back seams and under the sleeves.

Overall ('Surculotte' or 'Pantalon de cheval' or 'Charivari'): ample trousers for mounted personnel, often with buttons on a coloured stripe at each side, reinforced with leather at the seat, down the inside of the legs and often ending in a leather cuff at the bottom of each leg.

Shako: cap with a leather peak and reinforcing bands, generally bearing a metal plate, cockade and cockade loop, feather or pompon and chin scales. Introduced in the 1790s for light troops, it had spread to the whole army by 1808. The shako gave an impression of overbearing height to soldiers. It was also supposed to give some minimal protection against sabre blows to the head.

Shoulder strap ('Patte d'épaule'): in this book, shoulder strap refers to a piece of cloth on the coat's shoulder, usually of the coat colour and edged with piping.

Surtout: a very plain undress coat, single breasted, with long tails and usually of a single colour. Collars and/or cuffs can be of a facing colour. Very popular with officers.

Rank Badges

Foot troops, heavy cavalry, dragoons, gendarmerie, transport corps.

Officers:

Colonel: two epaulettes with bullion fringe.

Major: two epaulettes with straps and bullion fringe of contrasting metal, i.e. for a corps with gold buttons: silver straps and gold fringe; for a corps with silver buttons: gold straps with silver fringe.

Chef de bataillon: one epaulette on left, strap with

no bullion fringe on right.

Captain: one epaulette with thin strand fringe on left, strap with no fringe on right.

Captain and Adjutant-Major: one epaulette with thin strand fringe on right, strap with no fringe on left.

Lieutenant: one epaulette with thin strand fringe on left, strap with no fringe on right. Both straps have a red line at the centre.

Sub-Lieutenant: one epaulette with thin strand fringe on left, strap with no fringe on right. Both straps have two red lines at the centre.

Non-Commissioned Officers:

Adjutant: two epaulettes with red straps with two (gold or silver) lines at the centre. Fringe red and gold or silver mixed.

Sub-Adjutant: one epaulette with thin strand fringe on left, strap with no fringe on right. Both straps red with two (gold or silver) lines at the centre. Fringe red and gold or silver mixed.

Maréchal des logis chef (Chief Quartermaster, equivalent of sergeant-major in mounted troops): two points up gold or silver chevrons above cuffs.

Maréchal des logis (Quartermaster, equivalent of sergeant in mounted troops): two diagonal gold or silver chevrons above cuffs.

Drum-Major: two red epaulettes, gold or silver strand fringe. Gold or silver lace edging facings.

Sergeant-Major: two diagonal gold or silver bars above cuffs.

Fourrier: two diagonal gold or silver bars on sleeves above elbows

Sergeant: one diagonal gold or silver bar above cuffs.

Brigadier (equivalent of corporal in mounted troops): two diagonal yellow or white bars above cuffs.

Corporal: two diagonal yellow or white bars above cuffs.

Appointé (Lance-Corporal): one diagonal yellow or white bar above cuffs.

Rengagé (re-enlisted soldier): chevron on upper sleeve, one for each eight year period. Generally white on blue, green or red coats; blue on white coats.

Bars and chevrons were 23 mm wide, often with red (usually) edging, on the coats and coatees. The corporals, appointés and rengagés also had their rank badges on the waistcoat but 11 mm wide.

Light Cavalry.

Officers:

Colonel: five gold or silver laces set as chevrons at

Officer, 1st Cavalry Regiment, c. 1800. This was the dress of line cavalry regiments until converted into cuirassiers in 1803. Print after Hoffman.

cuffs and front of breeches, three of 20 mm wide, two of 9 mm.

Lieutenant-Colonel: two of 20 mm, two of 9 mm.

Major: one of 9 mm near the cuff, one of 20 mm and two of 9 mm.

Captain: four laces of 9 mm.

Second Captain: three laces of 9 mm.

Lieutenant: two laces of 9 mm.

Sub-Lieutenant: one lace of 9 mm.

Adjutant: three silver or gold chevrons above cuffs.

Maréchal des logis chef: two silver or gold chevrons above cuffs.

Maréchal des logis: one silver or gold chevron above cuffs.

Fourriers: three silver or gold chevrons above elbow.

Brigadiers: two white or yellow chevrons above cuffs.

Appointés: one white or yellow chevron above cuffs.

Rengagé: one white or yellow chevron above elbow per eight years of service.

Senior Officers and Staff

Napoleon Bonaparte was born on 15 August 1769. At age ten, he entered the military academy of Brienne and from then on wore a uniform during most of his life. First that of Brienne then, from 1783, that of the École Militaire in Paris. He was commissioned in the artillery in 1785 and wore its uniform until promoted general in 1794. From 1799 when he became Consul, and later First Consul, he often wore a scarlet 'uniform' coat embroidered with gold associated with that function but, as time went on, his dress became simpler and he reverted gradually to purely military uniforms. By the time he was crowned Emperor in 1804, he commonly wore the plain hat, an undress coat of the Chasseurs à cheval or the uniform of Foot Grenadiers of his guard and, increasingly, his famous grey greatcoat.

This simplicity in dress from the world's most eminent man of the day contrasted enormously with the lavish dress of his entourage, be they civil or military, and considerably enhanced his image and his legend. His hat, his grey greatcoat are still universally recognized instantly nearly two centuries later!

Yet, while Napoleon must have planned this studied simplicity in dress, his disdain of 'fuss and feathers' and his love of comfortable clothes were factors. His personal valet, Constant, recalled that he was not fussy about fashion but he liked his clothes to be comfortable and made of the finest materials. 'His frocks, his coats and his grey greatcoat were made of the finest Louviers cloth' but his daily dress did not vary much. Every morning, he put on white silk stockings, white casemere breeches or tight pantaloons, white casemere waistcoat, shirt, black silk stock and either the green undress coat of the Guard Chasseurs à cheval or, less often, the blue coat of the Grenadiers of the Guard. He would wear soft leather riding boots with silver spurs or 'short English-style boots'. The Emperor's famous hat was of 'beaver felt, extremely fine and very light; the inside lined with silk. It had no tassels, lace or plume, simply with a flat silk loop holding a small tricolour cockade'.

Under his uniform coat and over his waistcoat, he wore the red sash of the Legion of Honour so that it was hardly visible 'except for parades' when he wore it over his coat. On his coat, he pinned only two medals: the Legion of Honour and the Iron Crown.

Generals and Marshals

At the time of the Revolution, French generals

The young Corsican gentleman-cadet Napoleone di Buonaparte at the Brienne military academy, shown in the school's blue faced red uniform, the first worn by the future emperor shown in this evocative print after JOB.

The French Campaign of 1814. One of the most famous pictures of Napoleon shown wearing his famous hat and grey greatcoat. It captures the sombre mood during the invasion of France by the allies. Print after the painting by Meissonnier.

adopted some very distinctive uniforms of 'revolutionary fashion' featuring bunches of large tricolour hat plumes, high stand-and-fall collars, ample tricolour sashes, tight pantaloons and low boots. The basic uniform was blue with scarlet collar and cuffs, often with white cuff flaps, and decorated with much gold embroidery. This was regulated further in 1798 with generals in chief now having red and white sashes, generals of division scarlet sashes and generals of brigades sky blue sashes but all this could be followed loosely.

Napoleon being treated for a slight foot wound from a spent bullet during the 1809 campaign in Austria. Roustan, the Emperor's personal Mameluk in oriental dress is taking off the boot while three servants of the Imperial household prepare clothing and medicines. They wear a livery consisting of completely green caps and coats laced with gold, red waistcoat and breeches. Wherever the Emperor was in the field, a picket of Chasseurs à cheval of the Guard in campaign dress formed a perimetre around him. Print after JOB.

Napoleon and Marshal Murat during the 1805 campaign. Murat, famous for his outlandish personal uniforms, wears a white hussar dress with scarlet pelisse laced with gold. Print after JOB.

From 14 September 1803, generals were assigned three types of uniforms. The full dress uniform was a blue coat with scarlet collar and cuffs heavily embroidered with a gold oak leaf and acorn pattern on both sides of the front, on and around the pocket flaps and on the collar and cuffs; gold buttons. This full dress coat had no turnbacks and no epaulettes. The white waistcoat had a similar embroidery. The breeches and stockings were white on foot and blue breeches and black boots were worn mounted. A gold laced bicorn with a flurry of tricolour plumes completed this dress.

The 'undress' uniform was much more popular and soon became the only one worn for all but the most elaborate dress occasions. It was a blue coat with blue collar, cuffs and lining but with no turnbacks although cut away, embroidered with the gold lace oak leaf pattern as on the dress coat, gold epaulettes; gold buttons; white breeches and long boots. The bicorn was edged with wide gold lace and a plume border which was usually white for commanding generals and black for the others. Even simpler was the campaign uniform which consisted of an all blue coat with blue turnbacks, gold embroidery only at the collar and cuffs, gold epaulettes.

Rank distinctions were, for generals in chief: double row of embroidery on the collar, cuffs and pockets; white silk and gold sash; four silver stars on the epaulettes, the sash tassels and the sword knots. Generals of divisions had a scarlet and gold sash and three silver stars. Generals of brigades had a sky blue and gold sash and two silver stars.

Marshals of France were generals given that supreme title for their individual achievements. Thus, being a marshal was not quite a regular military rank although it was understood that he was the commander in chief of an army. The uniform worn by most of Napoleon's marshals was basically that of generals in chief but with additional gold oak leaf embroidery on the coat seams at the sleeves and the back. However, some just wore general in chief's uniforms in the field. Naturally, a marshal such as Murat would dress after his own outlandish taste and still be somewhat within a certain legitimacy as

Marshal Angereau in full dress uniform. Marshals usually had the same as senior generals with the addition of embroidery at the coat seams. Print after portrait.

Above.
M. de Vence, orderly officer to the Emperor, 1809. Print after painting by A. Adam.

Top right.
Count d'Astorg, Aide de camp to Marshal Béssières, 1812, wearing the regulation hussar dress for a marshal's aide de camp. Print after a portrait by Gounod.

Right.
Baron Lejeune, ADC to Marshal Berthier painted this portrait of himself proudly wearing the uniform he designed. Entering Madrid in December 1808 with five other of Berthier's ADCs, he later wrote that 'we were remarkable even at the head of the Imperial Guard... I never saw anything more brilliant or more elegant...than our cavalcade...' Print after self portrait.

marshal's uniforms were not officially regulated until 1836.

There also were a few special ranks such as Colonel-General of Hussars. The holder of this office was Marshal Junot which entitled him to wear a white dolman, blue pelisse and breeches, red boots, black shako with white aigrette, the whole richly embroidered, corded and laced with gold. The Colonel-General of the Chasseurs à cheval of the

Guard had a similar dress but with green dolman, red pelisse and breeches, and a fur busby.

Aides de Camp (ADC)

During the Imperial era, the number of ADCs was to be six for marshals, three for generals of divisions and two for generals of brigades. The Emperor had some ADCs at his service and also had up to 11 'Officiers d'ordonnance' to transmit his orders.

Uniform: early revolutionary ADCs tended to wear blue with sky blue collar and red cuffs and, from 1798, their regimental uniforms with an arm-band on the upper left arm of the colour of their commander's sash with gold embroidery. From 1803, the uniform was to be a blue single breasted coat, sky blue collar and cuffs, blue turnbacks with gold thunderbolts, gold epaulettes; gold buttons; white waistcoat; blue breeches and pantaloons; plain bicorn with gold cockade loop with white tipped red, blue tipped red or sky blue plume for ADCs of generals in chief, of division and of brigade. However, many wore their regimental uniforms instead or added details such as lapels piped sky blue.

On 30 March 1807, an order attempted to check the fantasy in the uniforms worn by ADCs. Those of generals of divisions and of brigades were only to wear a blue coat with long tails, 'sky blue collar and buttons of aides de camp' and a bicorn. However, some fantasy went on as engineer Captain Paulin, ADC to General of Division Bertrand, recalled wearing a pelisse, a 'dolman with astrakhan fur with the czapska' during 1809. Portraits of the period show many variations.

By the order of 30 March 1807, only the ADCs of marshals would 'be allowed to wear the blue hussar-style coat [dolman] with gold cords, colback or fur cap.' On 3 May 1807, the uniform of marshals' ADCs was further ordered to have a red collar and cuffs on the dolman, gold buttons and braid, fur busby in winter and shako in summer.

The order of 30 March 1807 also mentioned that princes commanding an army corps could chose the colours of their ADCs hussar uniforms. Some had already been chosen. The order acknowledged that the ADCs of Prince Jérôme had a green uniform with 'red facings and silver cords.' The ADCs of the Grand Duke of Berg, Murat, wore 'amaranth with buff facings and gold cords. White pelisse with gold lace.'

Other princes quickly acted to select their uniforms. By 20 April 1807, the Prince of Ponte Corvo, Bernadotte, had his ADCs in 'sky blue dolman with buff collar and cuffs, sky blue pantaloons, buff pelisse with all garnishing in gold.' The Prince of Neufchâtel, Berthier, dressed his ADCs in a 'white dolman with scarlet collar and cuffs, scarlet pantaloons, black pelisse, all the garnishings in gold.' From August 1807, Berthier's ADCs also had a simpler uniform consisting of a scarlet frock with black collar and pointed cuffs, white piped black lapels, facings embroidered with gold oak leaves, gold epaulettes, white waistcoat and breeches, bicorn hat with black plume.

Berthier was very touchy about his ADCs uniforms; General Castellane recalled that in Spain during 1809, Berthier insisted that only his ADCs would wear red trousers among his staff. Even the minister of war's ADC sent to serve with Berthier had to wear blue trouser. One day, one of Marshal Ney's ADCs arrived and 'presented dispatches wearing red pantaloons; [Berthier's] anger was most comical' and the unfortunate ADC had to immediately obtain 'with great difficulty' another pair of trousers before he could leave!

There were many other variations and changes but the example given above will give a fair idea of the fanciful and varied dress of the ADCs.

Last but not least, the uniforms of the Emperor's 'Officiers d'ordonnance' or orderly officers: on 30 March 1807, they were reported wearing a 'green coat with gold aiguillettes.' Possibly because of its resemblance to the Imperial livery, this was ordered changed on 31 January 1809 to 'a hussar style medium blue [usually shown as sky blue] frock [shown as a long tailed coat with pointed lapels] with cuffs, collar, lapels and lining of the same colour; cuffs, collar and lapels embroidered with silver; silver epaulettes and aiguillettes, scarlet waistcoat and medium blue pantaloons laced silver; hussar boots; bicorn hat with silver garnishing.' Dress housings were to be a hussar style tiger skin or bearskin edged with scarlet. However, medium blue cloth edged with silver was used for ordinary duty.

Marshal's Guides

Some marshals had their own companies of 'guides' which were escort units of light cavalry. They were usually dressed in luxurious and colourful uniforms. For instance, Marshal Mortier's had green dolman and breeches, yellow collar, cuffs and pelisse edged with black fur, yellow cords and buttons, green and yellow sash, busby with white plume tipped red, yellow bag piped green.

Opposite.

Marshal Josef Poniatowsky, 1813. Wearing a Polish dress uniform of blue with crimson trousers and silver lace. After a print published in Dresden.

LE PRINCE JOSEPH PONIATOWSKI
COMMANDANT EN CHEF DE L'ARMÉE POLONAISE
MARÉCHAL DE L'ÉTAT FRANÇAIS, CHEVALIER DES DIFFÉRENTS ORDRES

18 Senior Officers and Staff

Artillery, c. 1808.

The French artillery of Napoleon's armies was reputed to be among the most advanced of its time. The second half of the 18th century had seen dramatic progress in the materiel and the training of artillerymen in France, thanks to the system brought forth by General Gribeauval.

The one major irritant left in the 1790s was the persistent difficulty faced by commanders on campaign when private contractors might not bring too swiftly to battle lines the excellent Gribeauval system artillery. Shortly after he came to power, Napoleon decreed, in January 1800, that the drivers be militarized, formed into 'Battalions of the Artillery Train' and put into a blue-grey uniform. Blue facings were soon added and eventually, some variations were perceived. For instance, it seems sky blue was often used instead of a light blue-grey for the coatees and white piping edging the facings is also recorded. The figure in the plate shows the standard dress for the Train in about 1808.

Gunners of the French Foot Artillery of the Line regiments wore a uniform that was almost completely blue except for the red cuffs, turnbacks and piping. Apart from the change from bicorns to shakos in 1807-1808, the uniform remained practically identical until 1812 when the coatee replaced the long-tailed coat. Shakos usually had red bands and pompons but some sources also show red feathers. The gunner in the plate shows the dress worn about 1808.

Many regiments of Light or Horse Artillery were raised during the Revolution, proved to be useful and were appreciated by Napoleon. Being 'light' the dress of the Horse Artillery followed that of the light cavalry and featured hussar dolmans and breeches. The colours were in keeping with the more reserved character of the gunners being all blue with red cords rather than the outlandish styles worn by hussars. The Horse Artilleryman shows the full dress used in about 1808.

Guns were usually of polished brass, the carriages and limbers painted olive-green with hardware in black. Painting by Christa Hook.

Above left.
Captain Dreux-Nancré, ADC to General of Division Gudin,
c. 1809. Print after miniature.

Above right.
Napoleon in his favourite dress: the green trimmed red campaign coat of the Chasseurs à cheval of the Guard,
c. 1804. Print after Duplessis-Berteaux.

The Imperial Guard

The units which came to form, in July 1804, the Imperial Guard, had various origins. The Chasseurs à cheval had begun as General Bonaparte's Guides. The company of Mamelukes was a result of Napoleon's campaign in Egypt and certainly a most exotic unit. During the Consular period (1799-1804), the guard grew considerably. Napoleon clearly wished to create a dependable elite reserve that would be the envy of the Army and create emulation.

By 1804, the guard stood at 9,775 men. In 1805, it had 12,175 men; in 1806, 15,470 men; in 1809, 23,924 men; in 1810, 32,330 men; in 1811, 51,906 and in 1812 nearly 56,000 men.

So that emulation and respect be maintained, the guard was divided into an 'Old', a 'Middle' and a 'Young' guard from 1808. Thus, the prestige of the old units was maintained, even enhanced, and without prejudice to the newer corps which could still boast they were part of 'la Garde impériale'.

Back from the disastrous campaign in Russia,

Opposite.

Top left.

Trooper, Chasseurs à cheval of the Imperial Guard in walking out dress in 1804. Print after Édouard Détaille.

Top right.

Trumpeters, Empress Dragoons of the Imperial Guard, 1813. The mounted trumpeter wears full dress, the one on foot the undress. Print after Martinet. Anne S.K. Brown Military Collection, Brown University, USA.

Bottom left.

Front and back view of privates in surtout, Foot Chasseurs of the Imperial Guard, 1807. Otto Ms. Anne S.K. Brown Military Collection, Brown University, USA.

Bottom right.

Privates, Tirailleurs-Grenadiers, National Guard and Tirailleurs-Chasseurs of the Imperial Guard, 1809. Print after Marbot.

Napoleon tried to boost the Guard even more during 1813 when the establishment reached 81,000 on paper. But in January 1814, the Guard had in fact only 17,498 men bearing arms while decrees brought up the paper strength to over 102,000 men.

Following Napoleon's abdication in May 1814, some Old Guard units were retained in service by Louis XVIII but they rallied to the Emperor when he came back from Elba in 1815. They were dissolved following the battle of Waterloo during the latter part of 1815.

Cavalry

Grenadiers à Cheval

Horse Grenadiers. Originated in October 1796 as a company of horse guards for the legislative assembly; part of the Consular Guard on 2 December 1799; 'Horse Grenadiers' in December 1800; regiment in November 1801; four squadrons; vélites squadron attached from 1805-1810; five squadrons in 1811; disbanded 23 July 1814; re-formed 8 April 1815; disbanded 25 November 1815. Considered the senior cavalry regiment of the Old Guard.

Uniform: blue coat with blue collar, white lapels and white three-pointed cuff flaps, red turnbacks with orange grenades, orange lace shoulder strap on left shoulder and orange aiguillette with orange trefoil on right; brass buttons; white waistcoat and breeches; grey pantaloons on campaign; bearskin cap with brass chin scales, orange cords, red patch with white cross, red plume; white cloak with three orange laces and red lining in front; blue forage cap piped red with orange lace edging turnup and orange tassel; blue housings with double orange lace with grenade, later crown. Undress consisted of the all-blue surtout with orange shoulder strap and aiguillette, nankeen breeches, white stockings, silver-buckled shoes, deerskin gloves, blue pantaloons and Souvarov boot in winter. Black horses,

Horse Grenadiers of the Imperial Guard, c. 1804. Front and back views of troopers wearing the undress surtout. Print after Édouard Détaille.

Trumpeter (back view) and musicians of the Horse Grenadiers of the Imperial Guard, c. 1804. Print after Édouard Détaille.

whites or greys for trumpeter.

Trumpeters: sky blue coat and collar, crimson cuffs, lapels and turnbacks with gold grenades, white cuff flaps, gold lace edging collar, cuffs, lapels and buttonholes, gold and crimson aiguillette and shoulder cords; brass buttons; white waistcoat and breeches; white bearskin cap with sky blue patch with gold grenade, gold cord, white plume tipped sky blue; also bicorn hat laced gold and edged with white and crimson plumes; crimson housings laced gold; blue trumpet banner with gold fringe and embroidery; gold and crimson trumpet cord; white or grey horses.

Chasseurs à Cheval

Mounted Chasseurs. Raised during the Italian campaign in 1796 as the Guides of General Bonaparte, became Chasseurs à cheval of the Consular Guard on 2 December 1799; attained regimental strength in November 1801; four squadrons; disbanded 28 July 1814; re-formed 8 April 1815; disbanded 26 October 1815. The unit was part of the Old Guard.

Uniform in hussar style: green dolman with green collar, red cuffs, orange cords; brass buttons; red pelisse with orange cords and black fur edging; red and green sash; red waistcoat with orange cords; red breeches with orange cords, later buff breeches; boots edged orange; busby with red bag with orange edging, green tipped red plume and orange cords; green sabretache with imperial arms embroidered. For undress, green coat with green piped red pointed lapels and collar, red cuffs and turnbacks with orange bugle horns, orange aiguillette; brass buttons; red waistcoat with orange cords; green breeches with orange cords, green overalls with red stripes and brass buttons. Green housings edged orange and piped red on the outside with orange bugle horn and later crowned eagle; white sheepskin edged red. Officers: gold buttons and cords, epaulettes and aiguillette on undress coat.

Trumpeters: sky blue dolman with crimson collar and cuffs, gold and crimson cords; brass buttons; crimson pelisse with sky blue and gold cords and white fur edging; crimson and gold sash; buff breeches; white busby with crimson bag, crimson and gold bag edging and cords, sky blue plume tipped crimson; sky

Trumpeters, Horse Grenadiers of the Imperial Guard, 1804-1814. Watercolour by Lucien Rousselot. Anne S.K. Brown Military Collection, Brown University, USA.

Vélite, Horse Grenadiers of the Imperial Guard, c. 1805. Print after portrait.

blue sabretache edged gold with Imperial arms; crimson housings with gold lace chain edging and eagle, sky blue valise. For undress, sky blue coat with sky blue piped red pointed lapels, crimson collar and cuffs edged with gold lace, sky blue piped red turnbacks with gold bugle horns, gold trefoil, gold and crimson aiguillette; brass buttons; crimson waistcoat with gold and sky blue cords; sky blue breeches with gold and crimson cords.

Mamelukes

Raised in Egypt in 1799; created as a squadron of 240 men on 13 October 1801; reduced to 150 men on 7 January 1802; organized as a hussar squadron and attached to the Chasseurs à cheval. There were fewer original Mamelukes as time passed, Frenchmen replacing them. In 1813, after the Russian campaign, the 2nd company was reorganized with French personnel and was nicknamed the 'Mamelukes francais' - the French Mamelukes. Corps disbanded 1814.

Uniform: Napoleon ordered this unit 'to have the same uniform that the Mameluks wear' which seems to have been just about anything that seemed oriental to Parisians. Basically, they wore a low fez with a turban, a sleeveless vest over a sleeved jacket, baggy trouser which became very popular with army officers, all these items being elaborately embroidered. There was no set uniform colour but the fez was dark red with white turban, the baggy 'Mameluk' trousers being often red and the boots often of yellow leather. They were armed with pistols, a blunder buss and their oriental sabres. The 1813 French Mamelukes had few means but improvised an 'oriental' dress of sorts. The headdress, however, was not a fez but a plain black shako with a brass crescent in front and a white turban.

Gendarmes d'Élite

Elite Gendarmes. Created 19 March 1802; 632 men in two squadrons of two mounted companies each and a half-battalion of two foot companies; 456 men in two mounted squadrons only in 1806; disbanded 23 April 1814; re-formed 8 April 1815; one company strong; disbanded later in 1815.

Trooper, Chasseur à cheval of the Imperial Guard in the campaign dress worn in 1806. Print after Édouard Détaille.

Trumpeters, Chasseurs à cheval of the Imperial Guard, c. 1804. Print after Édouard Détaille.

Uniform: blue coat, red collar, lapels and cuffs, blue cuff flaps piped red, red turnbacks with white grenades; pewter buttons; white aiguillette; white trefoils on blue at shoulders; buff waistcoat and breeches; black long boots; bearskin cap with visor, white metal chin scales, red back panel with white grenade, white cords, red plume (white plume for parades); yellow-buff gauntlet gloves; yellow-buff belt edged white; white metal belt-plate with brass eagle; blue cloak with red cuffs. Blue housings with white lace and ornaments. Officers silver metal, lace and cords.

The Elite Gendarmes on foot of 1802-05 had the same uniform except for epaulettes instead of aiguillettes and trefoils, long black gaiters, bearskin cap with no cords, arms and equipment of foot Gendarmerie.

Trumpeters: red coat, blue collar, cuffs, lapels and turnback, silver buttonhole and edging lace; silver buttons; silver and red aiguillette and trefoils; bearskin cap with red plume with white tip; blue housings laced silver. Rest of uniform the same as the men.

Drummers of foot companies: red coat, blue collar,

cuffs, cuff flaps, lapels and turnback, silver buttonhole and edging lace, blue wings with white lace and fringes; silver buttons; white trefoils; bicorn hat edged with red and white plumes, red standing plume with white top third.

Dragons de l'Impératrice
Empress Dragoons. Regiment created on 15 April 1806; named Empress Dragoons in 1807; disbanded 12 May 1814; re-formed 8 April 1815; disbanded 15 December 1815.

Uniform: green coat with green collar, white lapels and white three-pointed cuff flaps, red turnbacks with orange grenades, orange lace shoulder strap on left shoulder and orange aiguillette with orange trefoil on right; brass buttons; white waistcoat and breeches; grey pantaloons on campaign; brass helmet with brass comb, black mane, panther hide turban covering also the visor, brass chin scales, red plume; white cloak with three orange laces and red lining in front; green forage cap piped red with orange lace edging turnup and orange tassel; green housings with double orange lace and crown. Undress consisted of the all-green surtout with shoulder strap and aiguillette, nankeen breeches, white stockings, silver-buckled shoes, deerskin gloves, green pantaloons and Souvarov boot in winter. Black horses, whites or greys for trumpeter. Officers: gold metal and lace.

Trumpeters: for full dress a white coat, sky blue collar, cuffs, lapels and turnbacks with gold grenades, white cuff flaps, gold lace edging collar, cuffs, lapels and buttonholes, gold and sky blue aiguillette and shoulder cords; brass buttons; white waistcoat and breeches; helmet with white or black mane and sky blue plume; sky blue housings laced gold; blue trumpet banner with gold fringe and embroidery; gold and sky blue trumpet cord; white or grey horses. There was also a sky blue ordinary duty uniform and surtout.

Gendarmes d'Ordonnance

Staff Gendarmes. This was not a police-type unit but rather a corps of orderlies to serve near the Emperor. Created 23 September 1806; four mounted companies of 150 men each, one 50 men infantry company; cavalry campaigned with the Emperor in north Germany and Poland; infantry stayed in Mayence. Recruited from youths from prominent families, it was resented by other units which probably led to its disbandment on 23 October 1807.

Uniform: coat completely green, of the same cut as the undress coat of the Chasseurs à cheval, without any other colour but green, turnbacks with no ornaments; pewter buttons; silver trefoil and aiguillette; red hussar-style waistcoat with five rows of silver buttons and cords; green Hungarian-style pantaloon with silver cords; hussar boots edged silver; also green overalls with silver outside buttons; shako with black velvet band, silver plate and chin scales, silver cords, white plume; yellow-buff gloves; black belts edged with red morocco leather and silver ornaments; green housings lace silver with silver eagles; same weapons as Chasseurs à cheval. Trumpeters: same uniform but sky blue collar, cuffs and lapel edged with silver lace; black busby with sky blue bag piped silver, white plume.

The infantry had the same but bicorn laced silver with white plume; black short gaiters edged silver; white accoutrements; infantry musket and short sabre. Drummers: same uniform except for completely sky blue coat with collar, cuffs, lapels and turnbacks edged with silver lace.

Chevau-Légers-Lanciers Polonais

Polish Light Horse Lancers. Created 2 March 1807; became Light Horse Lancers (Chevau-Légers-

Trooper of the Mamelukes of the Imperial Guard, fighting to quell the insurrection in Madrid during May 1808. There was no love lost between Spaniards and these 'Moors' with their arabic costumes and weapons. Print after JOB.

Lanciers) in 1809; 1st Regiment from September 1810; reduced to one squadron in 1814 which went to Elba; disbanded 1 October 1815.

3e Régiment de Chevau-Légers-Lanciers Polonais (3rd Polish Light Horse Lancers). Created 5 July 1812; nearly all lost in Russia; remnants merged into 1st regiment on 22 March 1813.

Uniform, 1st Regiment: two uniforms were prescribed in 1807, a white parade uniform and a blue uniform but the need for a white parade uniform was soon questioned and only the blue uniform was made. It was in the Polish style: blue kurta, crimson collar, cuffs, lapels, turnbacks and piping edging back seams, silver lace edging lapels, white aiguillette and epaulette; pewter buttons; blue trousers with double crimson stripes; czapska with crimson crown piped white, white cords, brass sunrise plate with white metal centre, white plume; white cloak with crimson collar later replaced by an overcoat with cape and sleeves; blue housingswith crimson stripe piped white, white crowned eagle and N in script, crimson valise

Trooper, Elite Gendarmerie of the Imperial Guard, c. 1810. Print after JOB.

Troopers, Empress Dragoons of the Imperial Guard, 1806-1815. Watercolour by Lucien Rousselot. Anne S.K. Brown Military Collection, Brown University, USA.

edged white. Armed with brass hilted sabre, carbine, pistol and, from December 1809, the lance with crimson over white pennon. For undress the kurta was worn with lapels buttoned over, blue pantaloon with crimson stripe and pewter buttons. Officers: silver buttons and lace. They also had a white faced crimson gala and ball dress.

Trumpeters: in 1807-08, crimson uniform with white facings, silver lace, white czapska. From 1809, white kurta, crimson collar, cuffs, lapels, turnbacks and piping edging back seams, silver and crimson lace at buttonholes on lapels, silver and crimson aiguillette and epaulette; silver buttons; crimson trousers with double crimson stripes; czapska with crimson crown piped white, silver and crimson cords, silver plate, crimson tipped white plume; crimson housings with silver lace and badges. Campaign and service dress: sky blue uniform faced crimson laced silver, crimson and silver aiguillette, white crown on czapska, other details generally as the men.

3rd Regiment: same as 1st but brass or gold buttons, yellow or gold lace and cords. Trumpeters had a crimson kurta faced white with gold lace; blue

pantaloons with yellow double stripes; czapska with white crown, gold lace, crimson and yellow cords, crimson plume.

Chevau-Légers-Lanciers de Berg

Berg Light Horse Lancers. Guard regiment of the duchy of Berg created 21 May 1807; the first squadron was denoted life guard; regiment admitted to the Imperial Guard on 17 November 1808; named lancers 17 December 1809; 2nd regiment raised early 1812 destroyed in Russia; one regiment in 1813; into Prussian service following the dissolution of the Rhine Confederation in October 1813.

Uniform, 1807- c.1808: white kurta, amaranth collar, cuffs, lapels, turnbacks and piping edging back seams; pewter buttons; white aiguillette and epaulettes; amaranth trousers with double white stripes; czapska with amaranth crown piped white,

Opposite.
Trooper, Empress Dragoons of the Imperial Guard on campaign in Spain, 1808. Print after JOB.

Drummer, Elite Gendarmerie of the Consular Guard, c. 1802.
Print after contemporary engraving.

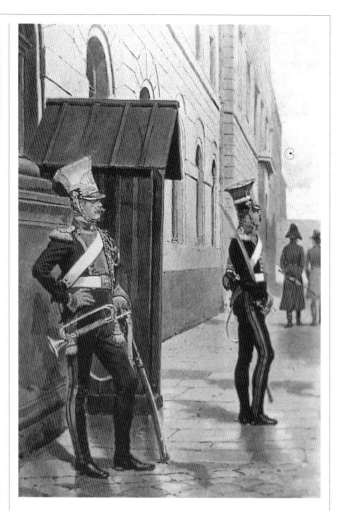

Trumpeter and trooper in service dress, 1st Polish Lancers of the Imperial Guard, 1807-1814. Print after Édouard Détaille.

white cords, brass sunrise plate with white metal centre, white plume; amaranth housings edged white. Life guard squadron had white lace at buttonholes and edging facings. Trumpeter had the kurta of reversed colours. Officers had silver metal, lace and sash around waist.

1809-1813: green kurta, amaranth collar, cuffs, lapels, turnbacks and piping edging back seams; pewter buttons; green trousers with double amaranth stripes; czapska with amaranth crown piped white, white cords, brass sunrise plate with white metal centre, white plume; elite company red epaulettes, busby with amaranth bag piped white and red plume; crimson over white lance pennon (in silk from 1812); white sheepskin edged amaranth, amaranth valise laced white. Trumpeter had the green imperial livery coatee with amaranth facings and livery lace.

Detachment in Spain 1809-1813 also had chasseur à cheval model uniform: green coatee with amaranth collar, cuffs, piping and turnbacks; white metal buttons; green pantaloons with amaranth stripe; red shako with white top and bottom bands, white plume brass diamond badge.

Chevau-Légers-Lanciers Hollandais

Dutch Light Horse Lancers. Former Dutch Guard Hussars, incorporated into the Imperial Guard and created as lancers, numbered 2nd Regiment, in September 1810; had four squadrons; six more Young Guard squadrons raised in 1813; disbanded 1814; re-formed 8 April 1815; disbanded 20 September 1815.

Uniform: scarlet kurta, blue collar, cuffs, lapels, turnbacks and piping edging back seams, yellow epaulette and aiguillette; brass buttons; scarlet trousers with double blue stripes; czapska with scarlet crown piped yellow, brass chin scales, yellow cords, brass sunrise plate with white metal centre, white plume; blue cloak; blue housings edged with a broad and a narrow yellow lace and yellow eagle and N; blue pantaloons with scarlet stripe and brass buttons. Officers: gold metal and lace.

Trumpeters: white kurta faced scarlet with gold lace edging; scarlet trousers with gold stripes; czapska with white crown, gold band, scarlet and gold cords, scarlet tipped white plume.

Young Guard Squadrons: reversed colours (blue

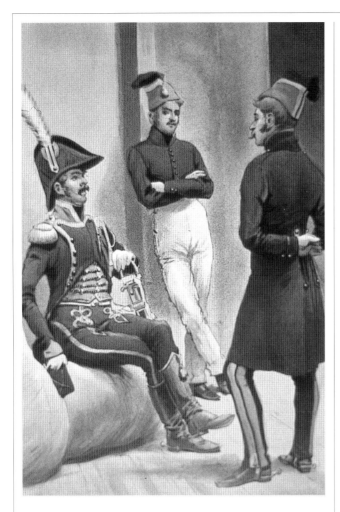

NCO and troopers in undress, 1st Polish Lancers of the Imperial Guard, 1807-1814. Print after Bronislaw Gembarzewski.

faced scarlet), greyish cloak; housings same but with only one lace. Officers and NCOs were from the old regiment and continued to wear the scarlet uniform.

Tartares Lithuaniens
Lithuanian Tartars. Created 24 August 1812; squadron recruited in Lithuania and attached to the Polish Lancers; many lost in Russia; remnants ordered incorporated into the 3rd Éclaireurs à cheval (Mounted Scouts) in December 1813, but the tartars appear to have remained distinct within the 3rd until released in June 1814.

Uniform of 1812: black astrakhan fur busby with peak, green bag with red tassel, yellow turban, brass crescent; green sleeved vest; red sleeveless round jacket trimmed with yellow cords; baggy green pantaloons with red stripe; red laced yellow housings, black sheepskin seat, Turkish-style saddlery; sabre, pistols, lance with red and white or red and green pennon. Officers had gold cords and lace. Uniform of 1813-14: black astrakhan fur busby, green bag, white cords, red plume; crimson sleeved vest; yellow sleeveless round jacket trimmed with black cords; baggy blue pantaloons; blue housings; crimson and white lance pennons.

2e Chasseurs à Cheval
2nd Mounted Chasseurs. Five Chasseurs à cheval Young Guard squadrons raised from January 1813; became known as '2e Régiment de Chasseurs à cheval'; disbanded May 1814; re-formed 21 May 1815 at four squadrons; stayed near Chantilly; disbanded 4 December 1815.

Uniform: green dolman with green piped orange collar, red piped orange cuffs, orange cords; red pelisse edged with black fur, orange cords; brass buttons; green and red sash; red or green pantaloons with orange cords; hussar boots; red shako with mixed orange and green cockade loop, black visor, company pompon; black sabretache; white belting; green sleeved cloak; green stable jacket; red housings edged green with white sheepskin seat. Officers gold metal, lace and cords.

Trumpeters (many variations): sky blue dolman, red collar and cuffs, red and gold cords and lace; brass buttons; red or crimson pelisse edged with black fur, gold cords; sky blue or grey pantaloons with double red stripes; red shako or black busby with crimson bag.

Gardes d'Honneur
Guards of Honour. Four regiments raised from 3 April 1813; recruited among the young bourgeois who were to arm and uniform themselves at their own cost; each regiment had 1250 to 2500 men divided into 10 squadrons; the 1st Regiment was posted at Versailles, the 2nd at Metz, the 3rd at Tours and the 4th at Lyon; disbanded 1814.

Uniform: green pelisse edged with black fur, pewter ball buttons, white cords; green dolman, scarlet collar and cuffs, pewter ball buttons, white cords; crimson and white sash; scarlet hussar-style breeches with white cords; hussar boots edged white; red shako with white top and bottom bands, silver crowned eagle plate and chin scales, visor edged silver, white cords, green plume with red tip for 1st Regiment, blue for 2nd, yellow for 3rd and white for 4th; black sabretache with silver eagle and regimental number below, 1st regiment also had scarlet sabretache with white lace and embroidery; scarlet sleeveless waistcoat; all green single-breasted stable jacket; green overalls with scarlet band and 18 buttons on band; green cloak; green forage cap piped scarlet; white sheepskin housings with green border. Officers had a bearskin colback with scarlet bag as well as the shako, silver lace and buttons, overalls with silver stripe. General commanding each regiment had the same uniform

Trooper in cold weather dress, 1st Polish Lancers of the Imperial Guard, 1807-1814. Print after Bronislaw Gembarzewski.

Kettledrummer and trumpeters in full dress, 1st Polish Lancers of the Imperial Guard, 1807-1814. Print after Bronislaw Gembarzewski.

with gold instead of silver buttons and cords.

Trumpeters: many variations. Green imperial livery coatee with chevrons on sleeves and broad lace on chest; reversed colours and red pelisse all with white cords; sky blue pelisse and dolman corded white with red cuffs and collar and busby with red bag; same as the men with, in addition, lace of the imperial livery on the pelisse and dolman, shako plumes inverted, black sheepskin housings.

Éclaireurs à Cheval

Mounted Scouts. Three regiments created 29 December 1813. Each regiment had four squadrons of 250 men each. The 1st Regiment was attached to the Grenadiers à cheval, the 2nd to the Empress Dragoons and the 3rd to the Polish Lancers. The first two regiments were half Old Guard and half Young Guard while the third was Polish. Half of the first two regiments had carbines, the other half and the 3rd had lances with crimson over white pennons. All were disbanded in later 1814.

1st Regiment uniform: the Old Guard squadrons had a green dolman with green collar, red cuffs, white

cords; pewter buttons; green pelisse with white cords and black fur; crimson and white sash; green pantaloons with red stripe and pewter buttons; black shako with red top band, red pompon, brass eagle plate and chin scales; green housings laced white and piped red. The Young Guard squadrons had the same but wore a green Chasseur à cheval coatee with scarlet collar, cuffs and piping, pewter buttons.

2nd Regiment uniform: green single breasted coatee with crimson collar, cuffs and turnbacks, green shoulder straps piped crimson; brass buttons; green waistcoat; green pantaloons with crimson stripe and brass buttons; crimson cylindrical shako, cockade in front with button at centre and orange cord loop, green pompon, orange cords, brass chain on leather chin strap.

3rd Regiment uniform: same as the 1st Polish Lancers but with white pompon instead of plume on

Opposite.
Trooper, Berg Lancers, service dress, 1809-1813. Watercolour by Herbert Knötel. John Elting, Cornwall, USA.

Top left.

Trooper, 2nd Dutch Lancers of the Imperial Guard, c. 1810. Full dress. Contemporary print.

Above.

Trooper, 2nd Dutch Lancers of the Imperial Guard, 1811-1815. Original uniform used on campaign. Musée de l'Armée, Château de l'Empéri, Salon-de-Provence.

Left.

Trumpeter in full dress, 2nd Dutch Lancers of the Imperial Guard, c. 1813. Print after Édouard Détaille.

czapska; white and blue stripped sash; grey pantaloons with leather inset; plain blue housing.

Infantry

Grenadiers à Pied

Foot Grenadiers Regiment. Considered the senior infantry unit of the Guard originating in 1796. Created on 2 December 1799 as regiment of the Consular Guard; numbered 1st on 15 April 1806; disbanded 11 September 1815.

2nd Foot Grenadiers formed 15 April 1806; amalgamated into 1st in 1809; 2nd regiment formed

Above.

Trumpeter, 3rd Polish Lancers of the Imperial Guard, 1812. Print after Bronislaw Gembarzewski.

Top right.

Officer and troopers of the Lithuanian Tartars attached to the Imperial Guard, 1812-1813. Print after Bronislaw Gembarzewski.

Right.

Officer's busby, Lithuanian Tartars, 1812-1813. Print after Bronislaw Gembarzewski.

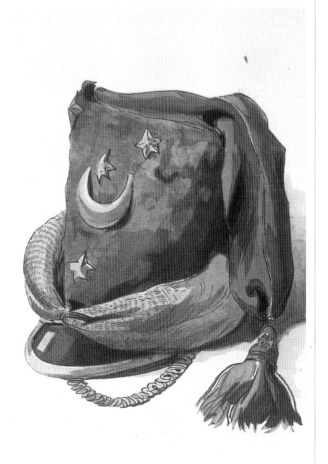

again 18 May 1811; disbanded 24 September 1815.

3rd (Dutch) Foot Grenadiers (3e Régiment de Grenadiers hollandais). Former Dutch Guard Grenadiers, incorporated into the Imperial Guard on 13 September 1810 as 2nd Grenadier Regiment, renumbered 3rd on 18 May 1811 when the old 2nd was re-formed; disbanded 15 February 1813 and amalgamated into 1st and 2nd regiments.

3rd (French) Foot Grenadiers Regiment created 8 April 1815; disbanded 24 September 1815.

4th Foot Grenadiers Regiment created 8 April 1815; disbanded 24 September 1815.

The corps had two grenadier battalions of eight companies of 100 men each per battalion, and a five-

Top left.

Troopers in full dress, 2nd 'Chasseurs à cheval' of the Young Guard, 1813. Watercolour by Lucien Rousselot. Anne S.K. Brown Military Collection, Brown University, USA.

Above.

Trooper in campaign dress, 2nd 'Chasseurs à cheval' of the Young Guard, 1814. Watercolour by Lucien Rousselot. Anne S.K. Brown Military Collection, Brown University, USA.

Left.

Back view of a trooper and elite company officer of the 'Gardes d'Honneurs' in 1813. Print after Marbot.

company battalion of vélites (191 men per company) added when it became the Imperial Guard in July 1804. From 1807, the vélite companies were amalgamated into the grenadier battalions. From October 1808, the number of companies were reduced to four per battalion, but 200 men per company, double the previous strength. During the 1815 campaign the Foot Grenadiers were organized into regiments of two battalions, each battalion having four companies of 150 men each.

Uniform: blue coat with blue collar, white lapels and white three-pointed cuff flaps, red turnbacks with

Above.

Private, Grenadiers of the Imperial Guard, 1804-1815. Original full dress uniform. Musée de l'Armée, Château de l'Empéri, Salon-de-Provence.

Top right.

Front and back view of privates in surtout, Foot Grenadiers of the Imperial Guard, 1807. Otto Ms copy, former C. Ariès collection.

Right.

Pioneer wearing the undress surtout, Foot Grenadiers of the Imperial Guard, 1807. Otto Ms copy, former C. Ariès collection.

orange grenades, red epaulettes; brass buttons; white waistcoat and breeches; white and black gaiters; bearskin cap with brass plate then bronze from 1809, white cords, red patch with white cross until late 1807 then white grenade, red plume; blue greatcoat; blue forage cap with white piping, orange lace edging turnup and orange grenade edged white in front; cartridge box with bronze-brass eagle and a small grenade at each corner.

'When we were under arms in full dress,' wrote Guard Grenadier Coignet, 'we wore the blue coat with white lapels, cut away below the chest; the waistcoat, breeches and gaiters were white; silver

Band of the Grenadiers of the Imperial Guard in the foreground, c. 1810. The Black cymbals player had a red cap with white turban, green aigrette and gold decorations, blue jacket with scarlet collar and cuffs, red trousers, gold lace and buttons. The Guard Grenadiers in full dress are behind. Print after JOB.

Foot Chasseur of the Imperial Guard, full dress, c. 1806. Print after Duplessis-Berteaux.

buckles to the shoes and breeches; black cravat lined white inside leaving a narrow white border at the top. In undress, we wore the blue surtout, white waistcoat, naked breeches and plain white cotton stockings. Add to this the pigeon wings [sideburns] and the six-inch [about 15 cm] long queue with its end cut like a brush tied by a black ribbon with loose ends of two inches long, more or less. Further add the bearskin cap with its long plume, and you have the summer dress of [the Grenadiers] of the Imperial Guard.' From 1809, a second uniform coat was issued instead of the blue surtout so that the grenadiers were always in regimentals thereafter.

When not wearing the bearskin caps, the grenadiers wore a bicorn with orange cords and red carrot-shaped pompon. This, until 21 May 1809 when 'at 11 in the morning,' recalled Guard Grenadier Coignet, 'we were ordered to cross the Danube and to put on our bearskin caps. The Emperor wanted to

present his old grumblers to the enemy in their finest dress. It was the end of our three-cornered [actually bicorn] hats. As we marched on the bridge in three ranks, each hurriedly took out his bearskin cap carried in a bag on top of the knapsack. As we were in a hurry to put [our bearskin caps] on, we threw our hats in the river. We never wore any [hats] since.' The bearskin cap was henceforth worn without cord or plumes except for dress occasions.

From 1812, the grenadiers also had on campaign blue winter and white summer pantaloons, worn over the gaiters. The blue greatcoat, single-breasted up to then was now double-breasted and the epaulettes were worn on it.

Sappers: same as grenadiers with red crossed axes on upper sleeves, red and gold epaulettes; fur cap with no plate, red and gold cord, red patch with white cross until late 1807 then gold grenade, red plume; from 1810, gold lace edging the facings.

Drummers: same as grenadiers with gold and red lace edging facings and buttonholes, gold grenades on turnbacks, red wings edged with gold lace, red and gold epaulettes.

A seasoned private of the 3rd Dutch Grenadiers of the Imperial Guard at right gives instructions to young Pupils of the Guard, c. 1811-1814. Print after JOB.

Privates, Fusiliers-Grenadiers and Fusiliers-Chasseurs of the Imperial Guard, 1806. Print after Marbot.

Musicians: blue coat with crimson collar, cuffs, cuff flaps, lapels and turnbacks, gold lace edging facings, gold buttonhole laces with tassels, gold shoulder trefoils on crimson; gold buttons; white waistcoat and breeches; black boots; bicorn hat laced gold with red and white feather edging and a standing white plume. From 1810, all crimson items were changed to scarlet.

The 1st and 2nd (French) Guard Grenadiers regiments both had identical uniforms with no regimental distinctions.

The 3rd (Dutch) Grenadiers of 1810-1813 had a different uniform. Full dress: white coat, crimson collar, cuffs, lapels, turnbacks and pocket piping, yellow grenades on turnbacks, red epaulettes; brass buttons; white waistcoat and breeches; long white gaiters; bearskin caps with no plate, crimson back panel with white grenade, white cords.

Sappers: same as grenadiers with red crossed axes on upper sleeves, gold and crimson lace edging coat collar, cuffs, lapels, turnbacks and seams; gold grenades on turnbacks and back panel of bearskin cap. Undress: white surtout with crimson collar, cuffs and

turnbacks, yellow grenades on turnbacks; bicorn hat with red pompon. Officers had facings of crimson velvet, gold metal and cords.

Drummers had the same white and crimson uniform as the men with, in addition, gold and scarlet lace edging the collar, cuffs, cuff flaps, lapels and turnbacks.

Musicians: sky blue coat, yellow collar, cuffs, lapels and turnbacks all edged with silver lace, white cuff flap edged with silver lace; pewter buttons; silver trefoils at shoulders; hussar-style fur colback with yellow bag having silver lace and tassel, white over blue plume; white waistcoat and pantaloons; boots edged with silver lace.

Chasseurs à Pied

Foot Chasseurs. Created 2 December 1799; numbered 1st regiment from 15 April 1806; disbanded 11 October 1815.

2nd Foot Chasseurs Regiment created 15 April 1806; merged into 1st in 1809; re-formed 18 May 1811; disbanded 11 October 1815.

3rd Foot Chasseurs Regiment created 8 April 1815;

Private, Voltigeurs of the Imperial Guard, 1811. Print after Martinet. Anne S.K. Brown Military Collection, Brown University, USA.

Private, National Guard Regiment of the Imperial Guard, 1810-1813. Print after Vernet.

disbanded 1 October 1815.

4th Foot Chasseurs Regiment created 9 May 1815; disbanded 1 October 1815.

Uniform: blue coat with blue collar, white pointed lapels, red piped white pointed cuffs, red turnbacks with yellow edged white grenades and bugle horns; green epaulettes with red crescent and fringe; brass buttons; white waistcoat and breeches; white and black gaiters; bearskin cap, white cords, green plume tipped red plume, no plate or patch; blue double breasted greatcoat; blue forage cap with orange piping; cartridge box with bronze-brass eagle.

Sappers: same as chasseurs with red edged green crossed axes on upper sleeves, green and gold epaulettes; fur cap green and gold cord.

Drummers: same as chasseurs with gold and green lace edging facings and buttonholes, gold grenades on turnbacks, red wings edged with gold lace, green and gold epaulettes.

Musicians: coat same as chasseurs, gold lace edging facings, gold buttonhole laces with tassels, green epaulettes with green and gold crescent and fringe; gold buttons; white waistcoat and breeches; black

boots; bicorn hat laced gold with green and white feather edging and a standing green tipped red plume.

Compagnie des Vétérans

Company of Veterans. Created 12 July 1801 for the old soldiers with over three years of service in the Guard. Company of 102 men raised to 200 in 1807. Continued after 1815 under the royal government.

Uniform: blue coat, blue collar, red lapels, red cuffs, blue cuff flaps, red turnbacks; brass buttons; white waistcoat and breeches; long white gaiters; bicorn with red pear-shaped pompon.

There was also a company of veterans attached to the 3rd Dutch Grenadiers but it remained in Amsterdam. Its uniform was the same as the Grenadiers except it had no lapels and had a bicorn with red pompon, yellow cockade loop and cords.

Fusiliers-Grenadiers

Fusiliers-Grenadier Regiment. Created 19 September 1806; establishment of 1600 men formed from the vélites; considered part of the 'Middle Guard'; disbanded 12 May 1814.

Veterans of the Imperial Guard, c. 1804-1815. Print after JOB.

Horse Artillery of the Imperial Guard, c. 1804. Trumpeter and gunners in various orders of garrison service dress. Print after Édouard Détaille.

Uniform: same as the Foot Grenadiers except for the following items. White epaulettes with two red stripes lengthwise on the strap; shako with white chevrons in 'V' on each side, brass scale chin strap and crowned eagle plate, visor edged with brass, white cords, red plume. Drummers had the same with gold lace edging the collar, cuffs and lapels. Officers had the same uniform as Foot Grenadier officers but with a shako having a black velvet top band with embroidered gold stars and edged gold, bottom band the same but without stars, gold cords and metal, cords worn until 1813 by officers.

Fusiliers-Chasseurs
Fusiliers-Chasseurs Regiment. Created 13 December 1806; establishment of 1600 men formed from the vélites; considered part of the 'Middle Guard'; disbanded 12 May 1814.

Uniform: same as the Foot Chasseurs except for the following items. Shako with brass scale chin strap and crowned eagle plate, visor edged with brass, white cords, green plume tipped red. Drummers had the same with gold lace edging the collar, cuffs and lapels. Officers had the same uniform as Foot Chasseurs

officers but with a shako having a black velvet top band with embroidered laurel leaves and edged gold, bottom band the same but without leaves, red over green plume, gold cords and metal, cords worn until 1813 by officers.

Tirailleurs-Grenadiers
Sharpshooters-Grenadiers. 1st Regiment created 16 January 1809; became 1st Tirailleurs Regiment 30 December 1810. 2nd Regiment created 25 April 1809; became 2nd Tirailleurs Regiment 30 December 1810. Each regiment had an establishment of 2000 men, reduced to 1600 men in 1810; considered part of the 'Young Guard'.

Uniform: blue coatee, blue pointed lapels piped white, red collar piped blue, red pointed cuffs piped white, red turnbacks piped white with white eagles, red shoulder straps piped white; brass buttons; white waistcoat and breeches; black gaiters below the knees; shako with white chevron, brass plate and visor edging, white cords, white plume tipped red; 1st Regiment had a red over white pompon; 2nd

Officer, Horse Artillery of the Consular Guard, c. 1803. Print after Hoffman.

Regiment had white over red pompon. Sergeant's shakos had red chevrons with two gold lines near each edge, gold and red cords, gold grenades on turnbacks. Officers had gold metal and cords.

Tirailleurs-Chasseurs

Sharpshooters-Chasseurs. 1st Regiment created 29 March 1809; became 1st Voltigeurs Regiment 30 December 1810. 2nd Regiment created 31 March 1809; became 2nd Voltigeurs Regiment 30 December 1810. Each regiment had an establishment of 1600 men divided into two battalions of six companies each; considered part of the 'Young Guard'.

Uniform: blue coatee, blue pointed lapels piped white, red collar piped blue, red pointed cuffs piped white, red turnbacks piped white with green eagles, green shoulder straps piped white; brass buttons; white waistcoat and breeches; black gaiters below the knees; shako with brass eagle, white cords, green pompon. Sergeant's shakos had gold and green cords, brass chin straps and visor edging; turnbacks had gold eagle

Napoleon takes aim with one of the guns of the Horse Artillery of the Imperial Guard, c. 1808-1815. The gunners wear the field uniform. Print after JOB.

inside and gold bugle horn outside. Officers had gold metal and cords.

Conscrits-Grenadiers
Conscripts-Grenadiers. 1st Regiment created 29 March 1809; became 3rd Tirailleurs Regiment 10 February 1811. 2nd Regiment created 31 March 1809; became 4th Tirailleurs Regiment 10 February 1811. Each regiment of 'Conscrits grenadiers' had an establishment of 1600 men divided into two battalions of six companies each; considered part of the 'Young Guard'.

Uniform: blue coatee, blue cut away square lapels without piping, blue collar without piping, red cuff with white three-pointed cuff flap, white turnbacks piped red with red eagles, blue shoulder straps piped red; brass buttons; white waistcoat and breeches; black gaiters below the knees; shako with white chevrons in 'V' on each side, brass scale chin strap and crowned eagle plate, visor edged with brass, red cords, red plume. Sergeant's shakos had red chevrons with two gold lines near each edge, gold and red cords, gold

grenades on turnbacks. Officers had gold metal and cords.

Conscrits-Chasseurs
Conscripts-Chasseurs. 1st Regiment created 31 March 1809; became 3rd Voltigeurs Regiment 10 February 1811. 2nd Regiment created 31 March 1809; became 4th Voltigeurs Regiment 10 February 1811. Each regiment of 'Conscrits chasseurs' had an establishment of 1600 men divided into two battalions of six companies each; considered part of the 'Young Guard'.

Uniform: blue coatee, blue pointed lapels piped white, red collar piped blue, red pointed cuffs piped white, blue turnbacks piped white with green bugle horns, green shoulder straps piped white; brass buttons; blue or white waistcoat, blue pantaloons; low black gaiters; shako with brass eagle, white cords, green pompon. Sergeant's shakos had gold and green cords, brass chin straps and visor edging; turnbacks had gold eagle inside and gold bugle horn outside. Officers had gold metal and cords.

Vélites de Turin; Vélites de Florence
Vélites of Torino, Vélites of Florence. Created 24 March 1809 by the Emperor's order; one battalion each; raised in northern Italy. These units were

Artillery Train of the Imperial Guard, driver, 1807. Print after Martinet, Anne S.K. Brown Military Collection, Brown University, USA.

attached to the Imperial Guard because of Napoleon's sisters. The Torino Vélites (Vélites de Turin) formed the guard of Prince Borghese, husband of Napoleon's sister Caroline. The Vélites of Florence were the guards of Elisa, Grand Duchess of Tuscany. In 1813, some French personnel from the Young Guard were added. Both units were disbanded 1 February 1814.

Uniform: Vélites of Turin: blue coat, blue collar, white lapels and three pointed cuff flaps, red cuffs, turnbacks and epaulettes; white waistcoat and breeches; shako with brass crowned eagle plate, brass edged visor, orange (later white) cords and red plume.

Vélites of Florence: blue coat, blue collar, white lapels and three pointed cuff flaps, red cuffs and turnbacks, white epaulettes with two red stripes; white waistcoat and breeches; shako with brass crowned eagle plate, brass edged visor, red cords and plume.

Gardes Nationales de la Garde

National Guards of the Guard. Regiment formed in Lille from 1 January 1810; two battalions of six

Sailors of the Imperial Guard, c. 1805, service dress. A Lieutenant wearing the blue undress with gold lace, epaulettes and aiguillettes is saluted by a Trumpeter. Print after Édouard Détaille.

companies each (four of fusiliers, one of grenadiers and one of voltigeurs); became 7th Voltigeurs Regiment 15 February 1813.

Uniform: blue coatee, white pointed lapels piped red, red collar piped white, red pointed cuffs piped white, white turnbacks piped red with blue eagles, blue shoulder straps piped red; brass buttons; white waistcoat and breeches; black gaiters below the knees; shako with brass crowned eagle plate, white cords, pompon of fusilier company colours: 1st, green; 2nd, sky blue; 3rd, orange and 4th, violet. Grenadiers red grenades on turnbacks, red epaulettes, sabre knot, shako cords and pompon. Voltigeurs had green bugles on turnbacks, green epaulettes, sabre knot, shako cords and pompon. Officers had the same uniform as those of the Fusiliers-Chasseurs.

Tirailleurs

Sharpshooters. 1st Regiment created 30 December 1810 from Tirailleurs-Grenadiers; disbanded 1814; re-formed 8 April 1815; disbanded after Waterloo.

Sailor of the Imperial Guard, c. 1807, wearing the full dress 'paletot' trimmed in the hussar style. Print after Martinet. Anne S.K. Brown Military Collection, Brown University, USA.

2nd Regiment created 30 December 1810 from Tirailleurs-Grenadiers; disbanded 1814; re-formed 8 April 1815; disbanded after Waterloo.

3rd Regiment created 10 February 1811 from Conscript-Grenadiers; disbanded 1814; re-formed 8 April 1815; disbanded after Waterloo.

3rd bis Regiment created 17 January 1813 from Pupils of the Guard; disbanded March 1813.

Foot Artillery of the Imperial Guard, 1810-1815. Print after Marbot.

4th Regiment created 10 February 1811 from Conscript-Grenadiers; disbanded 1814; re-formed 8 April 1815; disbanded after Waterloo.

4th bis Regiment created 17 January 1813 from Pupils of the Guard; disbanded March 1813.

5th Regiment created 18 May 1811; disbanded 1814; re-formed 8 April 1815; disbanded after Waterloo.

5th bis Regiment created 17 January 1813 from Pupils of the Guard; disbanded March 1813.

6th Regiment created 28 August 1811; disbanded 1814; re-formed 8 April 1815; disbanded after Waterloo.

6th bis Regiment created 17 January 1813; disbanded March 1813.

7th Regiment created 17 January 1813; disbanded 1814; re-formed 8 April 1815; disbanded after Waterloo.

8th Regiment created 23 March 1813; disbanded 1814; re-formed 8 April 1815; disbanded after Waterloo.

9th to 13th Regiments created 6 April 1813; disbanded 1814.

14th to 16th Regiments created 11 January 1814; disbanded later in 1814.

17th to 19th Regiments created 21 January 1814; disbanded later in 1814.

Each regiment had an establishment of 1600 men. However, this remained only a paper strength for the regiments raised in 1813-14; considered part of the 'Young Guard'.

Uniform: blue coatee, blue pointed lapels piped white, red collar piped blue, red pointed cuffs piped white, red turnbacks piped white with white eagles, red shoulder straps piped white; brass buttons; white waistcoat and breeches; boot-shaped black gaiters bellow the knees with brass buttons; shako with white 'V' chevron, brass plate and visor edging, red cords until 1813, brass chin scales from 1813; 1st Regiment had a red over white pompon; 2nd had white over red pompon; 3rd had red pompon with white centre; 4th had white pompon with red centre; 5th had white pompon with blue centre; 6th had blue pompon with white centre; 1st Regiment had red over white plume, 2nd and 3rd red plumes until c. 1813. Sergeant's shakos had red chevrons with two gold lines near each edge, gold and red cords, gold grenades on turnbacks. Officers had gold metal and cords.

From April 1813, the coatee lapels were square at bottom, ordinary shakos with no chevrons or cords with brass eagle and chin scales, red pompon.

The 1815 uniform of the 1st to 6th Tirailleurs Regiments of the Young Guard was the same but with red epaulettes for the grenadiers.

Voltigeurs

1st Regiment created 30 December 1810 from Tirailleurs-Chasseurs; disbanded 1814; re-formed 8 April 1815; disbanded after Waterloo.

2nd Regiment created 30 December 1810 from Tirailleurs-Chasseurs; disbanded 1814; re-formed 8 April 1815; disbanded after Waterloo.

3rd Regiment created 10 February 1811 from Conscript-Chasseurs; disbanded 1814; re-formed 8 April 1815; disbanded after Waterloo.

3rd bis Regiment created 17 January 1813 from Pupils of the Guard; disbanded March 1813.

4th Regiment created 10 February 1811 from Conscript-Chasseurs; disbanded 1814; re-formed 8 April 1815; disbanded after Waterloo.

4th bis Regiment created 17 January 1813; disbanded March 1813.

5th Regiment created 18 May 1811; disbanded 1814; re-formed 8 April 1815; disbanded after Waterloo.

5th bis Regiment created 17 January 1813;

disbanded March 1813.

6th Regiment created 28 August 1811; disbanded 1814; re-formed 8 April 1815; disbanded after Waterloo.

6th bis Regiment created 10 January 1813; disbanded March 1813.

7th Regiment created 15 February 1813 from National Guards of the Guard; disbanded 1814; re-formed 12 May 1815; disbanded after Waterloo.

8th Regiment created 23 March 1813; disbanded 1814; re-formed 12 May 1815; disbanded after Waterloo.

9th to 13th Regiments created 6 April 1813; disbanded 1814.

14th to 16th Regiments created 11 January 1814; disbanded later in 1814.

17th to 19th Regiments created 21 January 1814; disbanded later in 1814.

Each regiment had an establishment of 1600 men. However, this remained only a paper strength for the regiments raised in 1813-14; considered part of the 'Young Guard'.

Uniform: blue coatee, blue pointed lapels piped white, yellow or buff collar piped blue, red pointed cuffs piped white, red turnbacks piped white with green eagles, green shoulder straps piped white (green fringed epaulettes with yellow crescent also seen); brass buttons; white waistcoat and breeches; black gaiters bellow the knees; shako with brass crowned eagle, white cords, green pompon, red over green plume. Martinet shows green over red plume, red cords, white 'V' chevron on shako, red eagles on turnbacks. Sergeant's shakos had gold and green cords, brass chin straps and visor edging; turnbacks had gold eagle inside and gold bugle horn outside. Officers had gold metal and cords.

From April 1813, the coatee lapels were square at bottom; shako had no cords and plumes, green pompon only for all regiments.

The 1815 uniform of the 1st to 8th Voltigeurs as before.

Pupilles

Pupils of the Guard. Created 30 March 1811; nucleus was the former regiment of Dutch Vélites incorporated into the Guard as 'Pupilles de la Garde Impériale' composed of youths from 10 to 16 years old whose father or uncle had died on campaign. Napoleon raised establishment of regiment to nine battalions on 30 August 1811; reduced to four then two battalions in 1813 as amalgamated into other units; last two battalions were Dutch and took the orange cockade in April 1814 and went to Holland in June.

Sailors of the Imperial Guard, c. 1804-1815, manning a boat in service dress. Print after JOB.

Uniform: green coatee, green square lapels piped yellow, green collar piped yellow, green pointed cuffs piped yellow, green turnbacks with yellow eagles, green shoulder straps piped yellow; brass buttons; white waistcoat and pantaloons; short black gaiters; shako with white chevrons, green cords, yellow pompon. Pupils had short light muskets.

However, the 5th, 6th, 7th and 8th battalions wore surplus Dutch white uniforms faced green or crimson. From May 1812, the pupils in green coatees were to have buff collars and piping and those in white to have green collar, cuffs, lapels and piping.

Flanqueurs-Chasseurs

Flankers-Chasseurs. Regiment with an establishment of 1600 men created 4 September 1811; considered part of the 'Young Guard'; disbanded 1814.

Uniform: green coatee, green square lapels piped yellow, green collar piped yellow, green pointed cuffs piped yellow, red turnbacks with white horns, green shoulder straps piped yellow; brass buttons; white waistcoat and breeches; boot-shaped black gaiters bellow knees; shako with brass crowned eagle, white

Foot Artillery of the Imperial Guard, Russia, 1812-1813. Print after JOB.

cords, yellow over green pompon. Officers had gold metal and cords.

Flanqueurs-Grenadiers

Flankers-Grenadiers. Regiment with an establishment of 1600 men created 23 March 1813; considered part of the 'Young Guard'; disbanded 1814.

Uniform: green coatee, green square lapels piped yellow, green collar piped yellow, red pointed cuffs piped yellow (cuffs shown as green by Vernet), red turnbacks with white eagles, green shoulder straps piped yellow; brass buttons; white waistcoat and breeches; boot-shaped black gaiters bellow knees; shako with white chevrons, brass eagle plate and scales, red cords, red over yellow pompon. The men had no hanger. Officers: captains and above had the blue long-tailed uniform of the Fusiliers-Grenadiers; subalterns wore the green regimental uniform but with long tails, white pantaloons, black boots.

Bataillon Polonais

Polish Battalion. Created 5 October 1813, short-lived unit recruited to honour Poles in the French army; battalion dissolved in early November after battle of Leipzig (16-19 October) when its commander refused to retreat eastwards with the French army across the Rhine.

Uniform: blue kurta with red cuffs and short turnbacks, white square lapels, cuff flaps and epaulettes; brass buttons; white trousers and short gaiters; plain black shako with brass chin scales, white Polish cockade on upper front and red pompon.

Artillery and Auxiliary Corps

Artillerie à Cheval de la Garde

Horse Artillery of the Guard. Created as a company of Guard Light Artillery (Artillerie légère) on 28 November 1799; two company squadron from 8 March 1802; Horse Artillery (Artillerie à cheval) regiment of three squadron from 15 April 1806; reduced to two squadron on 12 April 1808; three squadrons from 13 March 1813; a young guard company added at the end of 1813; disbanded in July 1814; two squadrons reorganized 8 April 1815; disbanded 3 October 1815.

Uniform in hussar style: blue dolman with blue

collar, red cuffs, red cords; brass buttons; blue pelisse with red cords and black fur edging; red and yellow sash; blue waistcoat with red cords; blue breeches with red cords; boots edged red; busby with red bag, plume and cords; blue sabretache edged red with yellow grenade and later eagle with crossed cannons. For undress, blue coat with blue piped red pointed lapels and collar, red cuffs and turnbacks with blue grenades, red aiguillette; brass buttons; blue waistcoat with red cords; blue overalls with red stripes and brass buttons. Blue housings edged red with red grenade; white sheepskin edged red. Officers: gold buttons and cords, epaulettes and aguillette on undress coat.

Trumpeters: crimson dolman with crimson collar, sky blue cuffs, gold and sky blue cords, crimson and gold cords from 1806; brass buttons; crimson pelisse with crimson and gold cords and black fur edging; red and yellow sash; sky blue waistcoat with crimson and gold cords; sky blue breeches with crimson and gold cords; boots edged crimson and gold; white busby with sky blue bag, crimson and gold bag edging and cords, sky blue plume tipped white; sky blue sabretache edged gold with gold grenade and later eagle with crossed cannons. For undress, sky blue coat with blue piped red pointed lapels, collar and cuffs edged with gold lace, sky blue piped red turnbacks with gold grenades, gold trefoil, gold and crimson aiguillette; brass buttons; sky blue waistcoat with gold and crimson cords; sky blue overalls with red stripes and brass buttons; black busby, sky blue bag, gold and crimson bag edging and cords, sky blue plume tipped white. Sky blue housings edged red with red grenade or eagle.

Train d'Artillerie de la Garde

Artillery Train of the Guard. Created 8 September 1800; initially four companies raised to six; disbanded 1814; re-formed 8 April 1815; disbanded 1 December 1815.

Uniform: light grey-blue or sky blue coatee, blue piped scarlet square lapels, collar, cuffs, three-pointed cuff flaps and turnbacks, red epaulettes; pewter buttons; light grey-blue waistcoat; light grey-blue hussar-style pantaloons with scarlet cords; black boots edged red; bicorn with red plume, later shako with red top band, white metal eagle plate, visor edged brass, brass chin chain, red plume, red cords; light grey-blue cloak; cavalry model cartridge box with brass eagle on crossed canons, white sling with brass furnishings; short sabre like Foot Grenadiers, red sabre knot. Sergeants and officers had a long tailed coat, light cavalry sabre model Year XI.

Foot Artillery of the Imperial Guard, 1813, in action at Hanau. This illustrations gives an excellent view of the equipment and the back of the uniform. Print after JOB.

Marins de la Garde

Sailors of the Guard (often translated in English as 'Marine' but 'marin' means sailor in French. Calling them 'Marines' was understandable considering the very military appearance of these sailors wearing shakos and armed like elite soldiers). Created 17 September 1803; battalion 737 strong, divided into five crews; raised to 1136 officers and men in 1810; disbanded 30 June 1814 except for a detachment with Napoleon to Elba; re-formed 8 April 1815 to 84 and later 150 men; disbanded 15 August 1815.

Uniform: the sailors wore a 'paletot' which was a naval jacket. Blue dress paletot with blue collar and scarlet cuffs, orange hussar-style cord in front and edging the collar and cuffs; brass buttons; scarlet hussar-style waistcoat with orange cords; blue trousers with orange stripe and Hungarian knot in front; shako with orange bands and cords, red plume. The undress paletot was the usual double-breasted type, all blue, with orange lace edging the collar and cuffs, plain blue pantaloons. Armed with musket, bayonet and sabre;

Sappers of the Imperial Guard Engineers, 1810-1815. Print after Marbot.

black accoutrements. Officers wore the uniform of naval officers with a gold aiguillette.

Trumpeters had the same blue dress uniform as the men, the undress was sky blue.

Ouvriers d'Administration

Artisan workers administrative corps. Company created 15 April 1806; became 'Bataillon d'Ouvriers d'administration' on 24 August 1811; disbanded 1814.

Uniform: sky blue coatee, sky blue square lapels piped scarlet, sky blue piped scarlet collar, cuffs, three-pointed cuff flaps and shoulder straps, scarlet turnbacks with sky blue eagles; brass buttons; sky blue waistcoat and pantaloons; short black gaiters; shako with yellow top band, yellow cords, brass crowned eagle, scarlet pompon; musket and sabre; white accoutrements.

Artillerie à Pied de la Garde

Foot Artillery of the Guard. Created 12 April 1808; regiment of six companies (five of gunners, one of pontooneers); three Young Guard companies created 9 June 1809, other companies gradually raised and organized into a 2nd regiment in 1813 to serve with the Young Guard; disbanded in 1814; re-formed 8 April 1815; six companies of Old Guard, 16 companies of Young Guard, one of 'Ouvriers-pontonniers'; disbanded 29 October 1815.

Uniform from 1808: blue coat with blue piped scarlet collar, cuff flaps and lapels, scarlet cuffs and turnbacks with blue grenades; red epaulettes; brass buttons; blue waistcoat and breeches; white and black gaiters; shako with red top band, cords and plume, brass eagle over crossed cannons plate; blue greatcoat; white accoutrements; muskets with brass furnishings. The Old Guard companies had powdered hair with queues. The tip of the queue was in a small black bag ornamented with a small brass grenade. Red cuff flaps from 1809. From 1810, bearskin cap with black visor edged brass, red patch with yellow or orange grenade, red cords and pompon. Service dress: all blue single-breasted round jacket with two shoulder straps; long blue or white pantaloons; black short gaiters; blue forage caps piped red. Drummers: same uniform with gold lace edging the collar, cuff and lapels. Officers had gold metal and lace, gold aiguillettes.

Ouvriers-Pontonniers Company: same uniform as the Old Guard but had red lapels.

The Young Guard artillery had the same uniform as the Old Guard but wore the shako and, generally, blue pantaloons and black short gaiters. From about 1813, they had the short-tailed coatee and no epaulettes or plumes a year later. Grey greatcoat from 1812.

Sapeurs du Génie de la Garde

Sappers of the Guard Engineers. Company of 120 men raised 16 July 1810; augmented to 250 men in 1813; battalion of 400 men in 1814; disbanded later in 1814; re-formed 8 April 1815; disbanded later in 1815.

Uniform: blue coat, black velvet piped red collar, cuffs, cuff flaps and lapels, red turnbacks with blue grenades, red epaulettes; brass buttons; blue waistcoat and breeches; white or black long gaiters; polished steel helmet with brass eagle badge, crest and chin scales, black roll on crest, red plume at side. Equipment and arms same as Guard Grenadiers, brass eagle on cartridge box, red sabre knot. For working in trenches during sieges, the men had special blackened iron helmets and front and back plates for protection.

Drummers had gold and scarlet lace edging collar, cuffs, cuff flaps and lapels, gold grenades on turnbacks, red and gold epaulettes, red caterpillar roll on helmet crest.

Officers had gold metal and lace, gold aiguillettes.

Train des Équipages de la Garde

Supply Train of the Guard. Battalion of three companies created 24 August 1811; disbanded 1814; re-formed 8 April 1815; disbanded later in 1815. They drove four-horsed, four-wheeled wagons painted olive green with, painted on each side, the Imperial crown and below: 'Garde Impériale. Bataillon des Équipages. Compagnie no. __' in white.

Uniform: sky blue coatee, brown piped scarlet square lapels, collar, cuffs, three-pointed cuff flaps and shoulder straps, brown turnbacks with scarlet eagles; pewter buttons; sky blue waistcoat; buff breeches; black boots; shako with white metal eagle plate and chin scales, red pompon, white cords; sky blue cloak; housings of white sheepskin edged sky blue; white belts; short sabre like Foot Grenadiers. Sergeants and officers had a long tailed coat, light cavalry sabre model Year XI. The men on foot had sky blue pantaloons and black gaiters.

Canonniers-Vétérans

Veteran artillerymen. Raised January 1812 for Artillery of the Guard veterans; disbanded 1814.

Uniform: as the foot artillery but bicorn with red pompon, cockade loop, cords and tassels. The veterans wore the Old Guard's powdered hair with queue.

Infantry

The bulk of the French Napoleonic army was made up of regiments of line or light infantry, the infantry being the 'Queen of Battles' in days of linear tactics. It was certainly the most numerous of the many arms of service in Napoleon's French Army and the majority of volunteers and conscripts served as line foot soldiers.

Infantry of the line

The French Revolution of 1789 brought sweeping changes to the infantry of the line. The regiments were numbered from January 1791 while volunteer units of all sorts appeared all over the realm which became a republic in September 1792. With most of Europe declaring war on the Republic and marching across its borders, the cry of 'La Patrie en Danger' (The Country in Peril) went out and all sorts of units mobilized. On 21 February 1793, in a desperate stroke, the Revolutionary government abolished all distinctions between old army regiments and new volunteer units, ordered that numbered Half-Brigades be organized immediately by meshing a regular battalion with two volunteer battalions. It was an inspired measure which permitted the enthusiastic new young warriors to be taught the 'tricks of the trade' by seasoned veterans.

On 24 September 1803, the Half-Brigades were renamed Regiments; raised to four battalions each in May 1804; a company of voltigeurs created in each battalion on 19 September 1805; from 18 February 1808, each regiment to have five battalions (four on service and one as depot), service battalions to each have a company of grenadiers, one of voltigeurs and four of fusiliers, the depot battalion to have four fusilier companies, all companies to have 140 men including three officers. With battalion staff, eagle bearers and musicians, the regimental establishment totaled 3908 men including 78 officers; from June 1809, regiments in Italy and Germany were to each have two, three or four-pounders but this was cancelled in April 1810.

Apart from the numbered line regiments, there were temporary units such as the five 'Légions de réserve de l'intérieur' formed in 1807 from surplus conscripts. They went into Spain in 1808, lost 11 battalions at Baylen and the other nine were incorporated into the line infantry. In early 1810, seven 'Bataillons auxiliaires d'infanterie' were formed from men in regimental depots in France and sent into Spain becoming the 130th Line and 34th Light Infantry in 1811.

The number of regiments increased rapidly in 1812 by incorporating various units and even National Guards, reaching 156 regiments by January 1813; reduced to 90 regiments each of 1379 men (including 67 officers) in three battalions in May 1814. The infantry was reorganized into legions in 1816.

Uniform: the Half-Brigades of line infantry had, from 1793, the blue 'National Uniform' which was to be the same for all line infantry units. For a time however, the line infantry ranks were a two-to-one motley of the new blue uniforms of the National Guards with the old white uniforms worn by the seasoned veterans. The blue dress was the so-called 'National Uniform' and was worn throughout the line infantry by 1796. While details in cut and headgear changed, it remained basically the same from the time of the Revolution and was as follows:

Blue coat, red piped white collar and cuffs, white piped red lapels, blue piped red cuff flaps and shoulder straps, white turnbacks piped red; brass buttons. The lapels were fastened (by hooks and eyes) at the upper chest but sloped away below. Collars were high and hooked all the way up or sometimes left open in a 'v'. There were many variations to the above, for instance red cuff flaps instead of blue or no cuff flaps at all; vertical pockets instead of horizontal but always piped red but some colonels had taken off 'the red piping on the lapels' complained the minister of war in 1805. Turnback ornaments for fusiliers varied also going

Infantry recruits at training, c. 1805. The recruits wear the forage cap and waistcoat for drills. The instructors shown in this print are grenadiers. Print after Martinet.

from hearts, diamonds, stars, eagles and of course, regimental numbers, all in either red or blue.

White waistcoat and breeches, the buttons being of brass, cloth or bone; black gaiters with black leather buttons for full and service dress, grey gaiters for marches and some units also had non-regulation white gaiters for parades; black cravat for full and service dress, white otherwise; linen smock and trousers for fatigues; all blue forage cap piped red with red band on turnup; greatcoat of various shades of beige, brown or grey.

The headdress of fusiliers from the time of the Revolution was a black felt 'tricorn' hat but actually a bicorn bearing the national (from the outside) white-red-blue cockade with a yellow cockade loop. To this some regiments might have added pompons, ordered to be 'round and flat' in 1804, of a different colour per company which could be blue, red, orange, violet, etc., but there was no clear order in colours until late 1810.

By an order of 25 February 1806, the hat was to be replaced from 1807 by the shako but this probably went into 1808 as well. The shako was of black felt

with black leather top and top and bottom bands, chevron on the side and visor, brass diamond plate stamped with the Imperial eagle over the regimental number, cockade above held by a white loop, white cords, brass chin scales. Units added pompons and some even put plumes on the fusilier's shakos. Many had pompons with a small brush on top (a 'houpette') and the centre, usually white, with the company number in black or red. The diamond shaped plate stamped with the regimental number was most common but others were in the shape of eagles or rising suns. When shako covers, usually beige, were worn, the pompon was put on outside. From November 1810, a new sturdier shako, a bit higher and wider at the top with no side chevron (which had proven useless) was introduced. The shako plate was to be a brass diamond with only the number, no cords, cockade loop or plumes to be worn but the pompons were given an order: green, sky blue, orange and violet for fusilier companies 1 to 4.

The regulation of 19 January 1812 did not change colours but the cut of the coat made it now a coatee with short tails, a blue crowned N on the fusilier's turnbacks, and the lapels cut square and fastened (by hooks and eyes) down to the waist. The waistcoat was cut higher and no longer visible. The black gaiters

French Line Infantryman, c. 1801-1807.

Napoleon's French Army had an incredible variety of uniforms, yet, most Frenchmen performed their military service in the line infantry wearing the uniform shown opposite. The French line infantry did not have distinct regimental uniforms as in most other armies. All wore the 'national uniform' decreed for line infantrymen.

It consisted of a blue coat with red collar and cuffs piped white and white lapels piped red with long white turnbacks. Only the brass buttons had, in principle, the unit's identification number stamped thereon. With this, the men wore white waistcoats and breeches, long black gaiters going over the knees fastened with many small buttons on the outside. Except for the headdress, this basic order of dress hardly changed until 1812 when the cut of the lapels and long tails were changed and made shorter, the uniform's colours remaining the same.

The hat, basically a bicorn, was the standard line infantry headdress at some of Napoleon's greatest victories. The infantry that marched into Austria and crushed the Austro-Russians at Austerlitz in December 1805, possibly Napoleon's most brilliant tactical success, wore the felt hats. So did the infantry that defeated Prussia at Jena and later the Russians at Friedland. Although shakos were being introduced in 1807, many units do not seem to have had them until 1808. It was the only substantial change in the infantry's dress until 1812.

Infantrymen carried the M. 1777 musket, the small improvements to it decided in 1800 not being generally in service before 1809-10. It had a bayonet with a 406 mm blade. The black leather M. 1801 cartridge box held 35 rounds and was carried by a white buff shoulder belt which, for fusiliers, also had a frog for the bayonet. The cartridge box flap usually had no badge but often had a white linen cover. The forage cap was rolled under the box with the red tassel hanging out below. Only corporals, sergeants, voltigeurs and grenadiers carried hangers and had another shoulder belt to hold it which also had a frog for their bayonet.

The M. 1801 knapsack was of cow hide with hair outside with two, later three, straps to hold the rolled greatcoat on top.

The rest of the equipment was more informal with no set models. Water canteens might be of tin, glass bottles in wicker casing or a carved gourd. Kettles and pans were also much varied. Painting by Christa Hook.

Above.

French line infantry marching near Viloutina Gora, Russia, on 19 August 1812. The men have the new M. 1812 coatee except the drummers who still have the blue coats. Print after Faber du Faur. Anne S.K. Brown Military Collection, Brown University, USA.

bottom band, or also have the side chevrons in yellow, green cords, green plume with yellow tip or all green plume. From November 1810, yellow pompon. From January 1812, shako with double yellow chevron to each side, yellow-buff epaulettes with the strap piped blue, collar piped blue.

Sappers: every regiment had a squad of sappers, dressed generally as grenadiers with red epaulettes and crossed axes badge on the upper sleeves, bearskin cap with red cords and feather but no plate, and equipped with a long leather apron, white gauntlet gloves, axe with brass mounted handle. It was customary for sappers to grow beards.

Officers wore the same basic uniform as their men but of better quality. Their buttons were gilt, they had epaulettes according to their rank and also had, on duty, a gilt gorget with a silver badge, usually a crowned eagle. Their turnback ornaments were as the men but in gold, the battalion staff having grenades. They wore black boots instead of gaiters. Their bicorns had gold cockade loops and sometimes gold tassels at each end. Bearskin caps had gold cords, plate and cross on back patch. Shakos had gilt plates and chin scales, gold bands and sometimes chevrons too. Plume and pompons were to be the colour of their company or white if on the regimental staff. A favoured and comfortable garment with officers was

Top left.
Line infantry private, fusilier company, c. 1808. This soldier wears a private's uniform but is shown with a hanger, normally carried by elite companies and NCOs. Print after Weiland. Anne S.K. Brown Military Collection, Brown University, USA.

Top right.
Officer and private of the colonial Chasseurs de La Réunion, 1804-10, in green faced buff. Although a corps recruited among white settlers, some blacks were also admitted. At left, a chasseur company private of the 1st National Guard Legion at Port-Louis, Mauritius, wearing a most distinctive czapska worn by the chasseurs. Print after H. Boisselier.

Bottom left.
Chasseur, 1st Light Infantry, 1815. Blue uniform with only the collar, the pompon and the top of the gaiters in red, white piping and white metal buttons and plates. Print after Genty.

Bottom right.
Napoleon with line infantry grenadiers on his return to France in 1815. The army was dressed according to the 1812 regulations. The white royal cockades on shakos were soon replaced by the tricolour cockades which many men had kept hidden. Print after JOB.

the single-breasted surtout which could be all blue, blue with a red collar or with a yellow-buff collar for a voltigeur officer. A blue full-skirted double-breasted frock coat was another favorite in chilly weather as well as a blue cape. Mounted senior officers had blue housings laced with gold. Fusilier and staff officers had gilt-hilted straight-bladed swords, grenadiers and voltigeurs had slightly curved sabres.

Drummers had, in principle, the same uniform as the men in their company with tricolour or yellow or orange lace edging the facings, red wings edged with lace, a brass drum with medium blue hoops and white belts. The green Imperial livery was announced as early as May 1810 but it was not really in wear until 1812. It consisted of a green single-breasted coatee with nine buttons in front, red piped white collar and cuffs, green piped cuff flaps and shoulder straps, white turnbacks, livery lace with green eagle and 'N' on yellow background thereon edging the collar and cuffs, five wide pointed doubled lace on the chest, seven lace chevrons to each sleeve and edging the coatee.

Were there many exceptions and 'extravagances' to the above uniforms? It would seem that the answer is 'yes' judging from known surviving records. In 1807, grenadiers of the 45th Line sported sky blue coat collars and cuffs rather than red. Not to be outdone that year, the colonel of the 63rd Line required the officers of the regiment to have orange collars and piping. Sappers had many recorded variations, those of the 3rd Line going so far as to sport sky blue coats faced red and shakos with a large brass grenade badge!

However, the 'Nec Plus Ultra' of deviations went to drummers whom the regimental officers naturally wished to be as fine looking as possible. The 9th's drummers and bugler, c. 1803-1809 had blue coatee, medium green cuffs, pointed lapels, collar and cuff flaps, white and red lace edging facings, its band had a colourful uniform that included scarlet czapskas trimmed with white, scarlet coatee with medium green facings edged with yellow lace, white waistcoats, medium green pantaloons with white cords. The 57th's drummers had, in 1809, a blue coat with sky blue facings and wings edged with orange lace; shako with red plume and cords. The 67th's drummers, 1807-1808, had a yellow coat, blue collar, cuffs, cuff flaps, lapels, turnbacks and wings all edged with tricolour lace, red epaulettes, pewter buttons, black shako with red top band, pompon, short plume and cords, brass diamond plate.

White Uniforms

A curious episode was the attempt to dress the line

infantry in white coats. It was motivated by the difficulty in obtaining large quantities of indigo, a tropical ingredient necessary to make blue dye. In April 1806, a decree announced that the line infantry would be dressed in white and a regulation followed on 24 July directing 14 facing colours, one for every eight regiments, with instructions that 19 regiments would start wearing white coats in 1807. The 15th Line had been immediately dressed in white as an experiment and looked impressive to Napoleon on parade in Paris. But the bloody white coats of the 15th's dead and wounded at Friedland looked horrific. From that time, recalled Boucquel de Beauval, the 'issue was settled in favour of blue' no doubt helped by the discovery that good blue dye could be made in Europe without indigo. On 20 June 1807, a Napoleon 'extremely displeased with the white coats' ordered the blue uniform coats to be issued again.

The white coat had the facing colour or piping of the facing colour on the collar, cuffs and lapels depending on the regiment. The regiments known to have worn the white coat were: 3rd, green lapels and collar, brass buttons, horizontal pockets; 4th, green cuffs and collar, brass buttons, horizontal pockets; 13th, black collar, cuffs and lapels, pewter buttons, vertical pockets; 14th, black lapels and cuffs, pewter buttons, vertical pockets; 15th, black collar and lapels,

pewter buttons, vertical pockets; 16th, black collar and cuffs, pewter buttons, vertical pockets; 17th, scarlet collar, cuffs and lapels, brass buttons, horizontal pockets; 18th, scarlet lapels and cuffs, brass buttons, horizontal pockets; 19th, scarlet cuffs and collar, brass buttons, horizontal pockets; 21st, scarlet collar, cuffs and lapels, pewter buttons, vertical pockets; 22nd, scarlet cuffs and lapels, pewter buttons, vertical pockets; 30th, capucine cuffs and lapels, pewter buttons, vertical pockets; 33rd violet collar, cuffs and lapels, brass buttons, horizontal pockets; 46th sky blue collar, cuffs and lapels, pewter buttons, vertical pockets; 53rd pink collar, cuffs and lapels, pewter buttons, vertical pockets.

There were variations to the above. The 3rd was shown with green cuffs, cuff flaps and brass buttons; 17th and 21st, scarlet turnbacks; 33rd, violet cuff flaps and turnbacks. The existing white coats were worn out over the next couple of years. On 14 October 1808, Marshal Castellane in Spain wrote that a few detachments still 'had white coats' and commented that 'the Emperor had wished to give this colour to the infantry; [but] had renounced. These coats were dirty on campaign. In action, the blood was more visible which produced a bad effect on the morale of the soldier. The 15th of the line participated in this campaign [wearing] white coats.' By late 1809, Marshal Suchet reported that there were no more white coats and bicorn hats in the infantry. In Europe that is... Incredibly, the 66th Line in Guadeloupe had heard of the white coats, felt it was a good idea in the tropics and made them on the spot. A French officer was seen in Guadeloupe during 1807 wearing the white coat with blue collar and piping, brass buttons and a bicorn. Three years later the British invaded Guadeloupe and sketched the 66th in white coats with blue lapels and cuffs as per regulation, and bicorn hats.

Grenadiers d'Oudinot

Oudinot's Grenadiers was the generic name given to temporary corps gathering grenadier, carabiniers and voltigeurs companies from various regiments, the corps being under the command of Marshal Oudinot. Such corps were formed three times between 1804 and 1809. The first formation occurred in 1804 when five temporary regiments of two battalions, each battalion having three companies of grenadiers and three of voltigeur were assembled for the projected invasion of England but later went to Austria and Germany until

Voltigeur private, line infantry, 1812-1815. Original shako and greyish beige greatcoat. Musée de l'Armée, Château de l'Empéri, Salon-de-Provence.

66th Line Infantry, Guadeloupe, 1807. The officer at left wears the undress surtout, the officer at right has the full dress white uniform. Watercolour by C.C.P. Lawson after W. Loftie. Anne S.K. Brown Military Collection, Brown University, USA.

dissolved on 1 July 1806. The second formation was ordered formed on 2 November 1806 to have eight temporary regiments, the first battalion composed of grenadiers and carabiniers, the second of voltigeurs, and campaigned until dissolved on 5 December 1808. The third formation was ordered by the Emperor the same day, to have six 'brigades' each having six companies, considerably augmented from February 1809 to an army corps of 39 battalions divided into 13 half-brigades and was disbanded early in 1810. These temporary corps had their own staff of senior officers and even some temporary bands.

Uniforms: in principle, Oudinot's Grenadiers wore the uniforms of their own regiments but it seems that some added various distinctions, especially in the 1804-1806 formation. Long red turnbacks were added to the coats and coatees of some regiments, notably the 17th Light. Red cuffs instead of blue in some light companies was also noted.

Napoleon visits a bivouac during the 1814 campaign. The soldiers wear the 'pokalem' forage cap with grey or brownish greatcoat. Print after JOB.

Drummers of the 1804-1806 formation, or at least some drummers seen in Alsace, had a white coat with sky blue collar, cuffs, lapels and turnbacks, orange lace edging the facings, white piped sky blue cuff flaps, red epaulettes; brass buttons; white waistcoat, breeches and gaiters; bearskin cap with brass plate, white cords and red plume; brass drum with blue hoops.

Bataillons Coloniaux

Colonial Battalions. Four battalions created 16 August 1803; remained in Europe as depots for colonial troops, later for refractory soldiers; five companies of 100 men each (one of voltigeurs, no grenadiers); reorganized into battalions of four companies of 140 each from July 1810; amalgamated with colonial pioneers to form a two battalion colonial depot on 5 October 1814.

Uniform: in 1803, to be 'light grey-blue, unless there is in stores [cloth] to dress them in blue, and the light grey-blue coat to be established upon renewal...' Collar, cuffs and lapels red, white turnbacks; pewter buttons; white waistcoat and breeches; shako with white metal plate and chin scales, company pompons. Muskets ordered withdrawn on 25 November 1813, armed with picks only until late 1814.

Infantry Uniforms in the Colonies

The various French colonies had detachments of line regiments which put up considerable resistance until the last fell to the British in 1810. In the West Indies, these troops retained their linkage with their parent unit in France but in Mauritius and Réunion, the two battalion colonial 'Régiment de l'Ile-de-France' was formed in 1804 from detachments of the 15th Light and 18th of the Line, its uniform as the line infantry with the features for the troops in the East Indies listed in the 14 May 1802 decree on colonial uniforms mentioned below.

There had been light weight uniforms for colonial units in the later 18th century but this was swept aside in the disarray caused by the Revolution. During the 1790s, a few metropolitan line units were sent to the West and East Indies wearing basically the same heavy woollen materials as in Europe and soon adapted their dress to local conditions by adding linen or nankeen jackets and trousers to their kit.

The large numbers of troops sent to Haiti in 1802-1803 basically landed on this hot and fever-ridden island in woollen uniforms and bicorns. On 18 May 1802, General Leclerc ordered uniforms more suited to the area consisting, for the line infantry a blue coatee with red turnbacks, square white lapels which hooked down to the waist, three buttons below, dark blue collar without piping, pocket flaps with red piping, red cuffs piped dark blue and white cuff flaps piped dark blue; white linen pantaloon with instep; linen half-gaiters worn over the pantaloon; black felt round hat six inches high with a three inch brim, the left side held up by a cockade loop and button.

In France meanwhile, Napoleon also issued a decree on 14 May 1802 concerning the dress of the infantry posted overseas. The blue coats were to be the same cut and colours as the 'National Uniform' described above, but made of light weight wool lined with grey linen. Troops in the West Indies, French Guyana and Senegal had a white linen waistcoat with no sleeves, gaiter-trousers of white duck and a canvass smock with blue collar and cuffs. Troops in the French East Indies had a white or yellow nankeen sleeveless waistcoat and gaiter-trousers, and no smock. The blue cloth coat was to last three years in the East Indies, six years elsewhere, and all waistcoats, gaiter-trousers, etc., were annual issues. Nothing was said of headgear, some had bicorns or round hats, others shakos, notably in Ile-de-France (Mauritius) and La Réunion

Fusilier, 1st Colonial Battalion, 1807. All four battalions had the light blue-grey faced red shown. Print after Martinet. Anne S.K. Brown Military Collection, Brown University, USA.

Carabinier, 5th Light Infantry, c. 1805. Fur cap shaped like a peakless shako with a white metal plate, red cords and plume. Sketch after a document in the Musée de l'Armée.

which made them from blue material on bamboo frames.

Light Infantry

Light infantry was a relatively new type of unit at the time of the French Revolution, the 12 battalions being numbered from 1791. This arm was to grow considerably in the years to follow. By 1803, however,

the 11th, 19th, 20th, 29th and 30th had been disbanded. The same year, the Half-Brigades were henceforth named regiments. In 1804, a voltigeur company was created in each battalion. The 32nd was formed in 1805 by incorporating a Tuscan unit, 33rd in 1810 with Dutch personnel; 34th in 1811 from auxiliary battalions in Spain, while the 11th and 29th were re-raised; 35th to 38th raised in 1813; reduced to

Sapper, Grenadiers d'Oudinot, c. 1806. The coat has the distinctive red turnbacks usually adopted by this elite formation. Print after contemporary watercolour.

15 regiments in May 1814; incorporated into the Departmental Legions from July 1815.

Uniform: from 1793, blue coat, blue piped white pointed (square from 1812) lapels, turnbacks and cuffs, red piped white collar and cuff flaps; brass buttons initially but later changed to pewter. The cut was the same as for the line infantry. There were some variations: the cuff was sometimes pointed with no

cuff flap which became the regulation cuff in 1812; cuff flaps might have four instead of the usual three buttons. Buff collar for voltigeurs from 1804. Shoulder straps were blue piped white for fusiliers, red epaulettes for carabiniers, green with yellow crescent for voltigeurs who also had a buff collar. From 1812, buff piped blue shoulder straps for voltigeurs, scarlet piped red for carabiniers. Turnback ornaments were white bugle horns for fusiliers, buff for voltigeurs, red grenades for carabiniers.

The waistcoat was to be blue piped white but was occasionally plain blue or plain white. Blue pantaloons; black half gaiters with white, buff or red (for carabiniers) edging. Beige greatcoat from 1806. Bicorn hat until 1801, shako thereafter.

Early shakos had a brass bugle horn plate in front, green cords, cockade on upper left side, plume above, usually green or green tipped yellow, red cords and plumes for carabiniers, often had wings in red for carabiniers or buff for voltigeurs as late as 1810. From 1806, shakos had plumes and/or pompons and cockades placed in front, white metal plate and chin scales, often with red or yellow bands for elite companies. Carabiniers had bearskin caps with red plumes and cords for dress, some units had busbies with red bags, cords and plumes until 1812, shako only thereafter the same as line infantry but with white metal plate and chin scales.

Officers had the same dress as their men and as related for line infantry officers but with silver metal and lace.

When stationed at Corfu, the 14th also had a uniform for the very hot summer weather: white jacket; pewter buttons; white pantaloons; black shako with a wing or 'flame' wrapped around it. Chasseurs had blue collar and cuffs, green epaulettes with red crescent, sky blue wing on shako with green plume. Voltigeurs, yellow collar and cuffs, epaulettes with yellow strap and green fringes, yellow shako wing, green plume tipped yellow. Carabiniers, red collar, cuffs, epaulettes, shako wing and plume.

Drummers of Light Infantry regiments had, like the line infantry, the same uniform as the men in their company with, in principle, tricolour or yellow or orange lace edging the facings, red wings edged with lace, a brass drum with medium blue hoops and white belts. The green Imperial livery was introduced from 1812. In practice, there were also many exceptions to the official uniforms.

Tirailleurs Corses

Corsican Sharpshooters. Battalion created 8 July 1802 as 3rd of the 'Chasseurs corses'; merged into 8th Light

Infantry in May 1803 but independent unit again from April 1804 as 'Tirailleurs corses'; recruited in Corsica but depot at Antibes; battalion ten companies (eight chasseurs, one carabiniers, one voltigeurs) reduced to six by September 1810; amalgamated into 11th Light from 8 September 1811.

Uniform: initially the standard blue light infantry dress; with possibly green pointed lapels and turnbacks from c. 1808; pewter buttons; black light infantry gaiters edged yellow; shako with white metal plate and chin scales. Voltigeurs had yellow epaulette, yellow top shako band, plume and cords; Chasseurs had yellow epaulettes with green fringes, green top shako band, cords and pompon. Tan or black Corsican style cartridge 'belly' box on tan waistbelt, tan shoulder belt over right shoulder only for short sabre and bayonet.

The colour of the coatee, waistcoat and breeches from 1805 has been given as brown by various turn of the century authors and artists (Quinto Cenni, not always reliable, seems to have been the first). However, archival research (A. Rigondeau in *La Sabretache*, 1973, pp. 163-164) reveals the battalion used blue and red material and white piping, the standard light infantry uniform material colours, in 1805; a May 1808 inspection reported again the blue, red and white material as before, but also green which may have been used for facings. The brown uniforms may have existed but there is no official record of them.

Légion Corse

Corsican Legion. Originally five independent light infantry battalion each having a carabinier company and four chasseur companies raised from 1802; grouped into a Corsican Legion in 1805; passed into Neapolitan service on 30 June 1806 except for 3rd Battalion which had remained independent and became 'Tirailleurs corses'.

Uniform from 1802-05: brown coatee with brown turnbacks with battalion facings (see below); pewter buttons; brown waistcoat and pantaloons; brown light infantry gaiters; shako. Accoutrements probably as Tirailleurs corses. 1st Battalion had red piped yellow collar and cuffs, yellow piped blue lapels; 2d, blue piped pink collar and cuffs, pink piped blue lapels; 3rd, blue piped orange collar and cuffs, orange piped blue lapels; 4th, green piped red collar and cuffs, red piped green lapels; 5th, blue piped dark pink collar and cuffs, dark pink piped blue lapels.

The 1805 Corsican Legion was to have a sky blue faced yellow uniform but the material was not available and Prince Eugène de Beauharnais directed in September 1805 that it be issued the standard light infantry uniform instead.

Bataillon des Déserteurs Français Rentrés

Battalion of Repatriated French Deserters. Created 23 March1802; called 'Chasseurs français rentrés' from 1809, 'Militaires français rentrés' from 1812; five-company battalion raised to six in 1809; stationed at Flushing on Walcheren Island; almost destroyed during British capture of island; reorganized in 1810; 1813-1814 campaigns, disbanded in August 1814.

Uniform: sky blue coatee, blue collar, cuffs, lapels and turnbacks, green epaulettes; brass buttons; white waistcoat; sky blue breeches; black gaiters; plain shako with cockade, green pompon and brass chin scales.

Chasseurs Corses

Corsican Chasseurs. Raised from about 1806; three battalions (Liamone, 1st and 2nd Golo); served in Corsica; isolated actions mostly against British naval raiders; incorporated into the Régiment de la Méditéranée and the Gendarmerie in late 1810.

Uniform: the light infantry uniform or a brown uniform with accoutrements as Tirailleurs corses.

Chasseurs corses raised again in October 1814 by royal government and reorganized by Napoleon's order from 23 March 1815 into four battalions each having a company of grenadiers, one of voltigeurs and four of chasseurs; disbanded after Waterloo.

Uniform: basically the same as the October 1814 formation with new facings for new 3rd and 4th battalions. Brown light infantry coatee, brown turnbacks; pewter buttons; brown waistcoat and pantaloons; black half gaiters; plain black shako with only cockade and pompon; black accoutrements. 1st Battalion, brown collar, green cuffs; 2nd, green collar and brown cuffs; 3rd, yellow cuffs brown collar; 4th, sky blue collar and cuffs.

Chasseurs de Montagne

Mountain Chasseurs. Created 6 August 1808; was to have 34 companies divided into eight battalions but recruiting proved difficult and the unit eventually had 4600 chasseurs in three battalions; made up of mountaineers from the Pyrenees; served in Pyrenees and northern Spain, mostly against guerrillas; disbanded late 1813 and early 1814, the men incorporated in the 116th Line and 4th and 25th Light Infantry. Re-raised from 9 May 1815, to have nine battalions; by 15 June, seven battalions raised totaling 143 officers and 3143 chasseurs, eight battalion raising in Bordeaux; all disbanded after Waterloo.

Uniform: procured locally and had many

Light Infantry voltigeurs and carabiniers in action, c. 1807-1812. U.S. Military Academy Museum, West Point.

variations; basically a brown coatee with sky blue collar, pointed cuffs, lapels and piping, brown turnbacks; white metal buttons; brown waistcoat and breeches; black half gaiters; black shako with white metal plate and chin scales, white pompon, red plumes and cords for elite. Brown lapels piped sky blue; brown lapels and collar piped sky blue with sky blue cuffs; red collar with red epaulettes (apparently for elite companies); white trousers; brown or grey-blue blanket roll instead of knapsack also shown. Officers had silver metal, black shako with silver top and bottom bands, plate and chin scales; long-tailed coats; sky blue trousers with brown stripe or brown trousers and gaiters. Elite company officer in full dress with fur busby, sky blue bag with silver tassel, silver cords and chin scales, white pompon, brown coatee with sky blue cuffs, collar and piping; silver buttons; brown waistcoat edged with silver lace; brown Hungarian-style breeches ornamented with silver; black boots edged silver.

Chasseurs des Alpes

Chasseurs of the Alps. Battalion raised in 1813 for service in south-eastern alpine region; disbanded 1814; re-formed from 5 May 1815; one battalion of 422 men by 15 June; participated in successful defense of Briançon; disbanded later in 1815.

Uniform: as light infantry but yellow piped blue collar, yellow piping edging lapels, pointed cuffs, shoulder straps and turnbacks.

Chasseurs Coloniaux

Colonial Chasseurs. Battalion created 26 May 1815, raised in Bordeaux with volunteer 'men of colour' living in France; organized as a light infantry battalion; disbanded following the 'insurrection' and pitched battle of a large detachment of these Black soldiers against the local National Guard and Gendarmerie at Agens on 23 July 1815.

Uniform: 'to be imperial blue and have the same cut as that of the light infantry'.

Légion de l'Ouest

Western Legion. Created 5 June 1815; four light infantry battalion; recruited with veterans in departments of Vendée, Sèvres. Loire and Maine area for local service. Probably had only started its organization when news of Waterloo reached western

France and disbanded.

Uniform: 'same as that of the light infantry, except that the collar of the coatee will be white. In the voltigeur companies, the collar will be yellow. Pay, accoutrements and arms will be the same as in the light infantry.'

Light Infantry Colonial uniforms

The light infantry units in the colonies had the same features decreed on 14 May 1802 for the dress of the infantry in the colonies (see that section) but with light infantry uniform coatees. This would have been the uniform worn by the 3rd battalion of the 18th Light Infantry embarking for Mauritius in November 1802. The light infantry uniform with colonial features may have been worn by the 1803-1810 company of Black 'Chasseurs volontaires de la Martinique' and the 1803-1809 two-company 'Légion coloniale de Chasseurs' which was part of the French garrison of the city of Santo Domingo (now the Dominican Republic).

However, the uniform of French light infantry in Saint-Domingue (Haiti) ordered by General Leclerc on 18 May 1802 was a blue coatee with blue piped red square lapels closed in front with three buttons below, blue piped red pointed cuffs, vertical pockets piped red; pewter buttons; white pantaloon with instep; white half-gaiters; black felt round hat six inches high with a three inch brim, the left side held up by a cockade loop and button.

Chasseurs de la Réunion

Created on 2 November 1803, to be raised amongst white inhabitants of the Indian Ocean island colonies of La Réunion and Mauritius; Black artillerymen were added in 1804; battalion 387 strong in 1810; 4 October 1810, three companies of 100 men each of Sepoys created and attached to the battalion.

Uniform: green coatee, lapels and turnbacks, buff

Light Infantry on campaign, c. 1812. The cartridge box is protected by a linen cover. Print after Raffet.

collar and cuffs, white epaulettes; pewter buttons; yellow or white nankeen waistcoat and breeches; black or blue short gaiters; white cravat; shako. Officers had the same uniform but long tailed coat, hussar boots and silver buttons and epaulettes. Gunners' uniform uncertain. The 1810 Sepoys were to have a cloth coatee (colours not mentioned), a nankeen undress coatee, nankeen waistcoat and trousers.

66 Heavy Cavalry

Heavy Cavalry

Carabiniers

The corps of Carabiniers, originally raised by Louis XIV as heavy cavalry armed with rifled carbines, consisted of two regiments of 820 men each at the time of the Empire. They were considered the elite of the heavy cavalry.

Uniform: blue coat with blue piped red collar, red cuffs, lapels and turnback with white grenades, red epaulettes with the strap edged white, red cuff flaps for the 1st Regiment, blue piped red for the 2nd; pewter buttons; white waistcoat; buff breeches; high boots; black bearskin cap, white cords, red patch with white cross, red plume, white metal chin scales from 1809; yellow-buff belts edged white; white gauntlet gloves; blue cloaks; blue housings with double white lace, white grenade, white sheepskin edged red. White long gaiters for service on foot; blue overalls for undress. Armed with a dragoon musket with bayonet and sword. The regiments rode black horses, trumpeters greys.

Trumpeters: reversed colours, red coat with red collar, blue edged silver cuffs, lapels and turnbacks, silver and blue epaulettes. Other items as above.

On 24 December 1809, the uniform was ordered changed by Napoleon but it took over a year to replace the old uniforms, which the men loved, with a flamboyant new dress finally in wear by 1811: white coatee, single breasted, with blue piped white collar and turnbacks, white grenades on turnbacks, red piped white cuffs and white piped sky blue cuff flaps for the 1st Regiment, sky blue piped white cuffs and cuff flaps for 2nd Regiment, red epaulettes with strap edged white; pewter buttons; white sleeveless waistcoat; buff breeches; sky blue stable jacket; grey overalls; high boots; brass helmet with white metal comb, chin scales and plate, red caterpillar crest; brass cuirass with front and back plate edged with white metal trim fixed with brass rivets, blue lining piped white; white cloak; sky blue housings with double white lace. Officers had silver metal and epaulettes; their cuirass and helmets were red-copper and silver plated with a silver sun badge with a gold circle bearing a star on the upper front plate; blue cloaks; sky blue housings with double silver lace, silver grenade, white sheepskin edged sky blue.

Trumpeters from 1811: for 1st Regiment, sky blue

Right.

Chef d'escadron Tarbé, 2nd Carabiniers Regiment, 1807-1810.
Print after portrait.

Opposite.

NCO Marteau, 1st Carabiniers Regiment, c. 1809. Print after contemporary self portrait.

GUILLOT SOUS OFFICIER
DE
CARABINIERS CUIRASSES

Top left.
Carabinier's cuirass and helmet, c. 1810-1815. Christopher Ross, New York.

Above.
NCO Guillot, 1st Carabiniers Regiment, 1813, wearing the undress sky blue surtout. Print after contemporary self portrait.

Left.
Carabiniers at the outskirts of Moscow, 1812. Print after JOB.

coatee, single breasted, six white laces on chest, white cuffs, sky blue piped white collar , white turnbacks with sky blue grenades, white epaulettes, helmet as the men but with white caterpillar crest; 2nd Regiment, coatee as 1st with, in addition, six points up chevrons on each sleeve, silver lace edging collar, sky blue caterpillar crest on helmet; pewter buttons and red trumpet cords for both units. From 1813, green coatee with sky blue collar and turnbacks with silver grenades, red cuffs and green cuff flaps for 1st

Opposite.
NCO Marteau, 1st Carabiniers Regiment, c. 1810-1811, wearing the new white uniform. Print after contemporary self portrait.

Cuirassier officer, c. 1804-1815. Note the white plume indicating a senior regimental officer. Print after period watercolour.

Regiment, sky blue cuffs with sky blue piped white cuff flaps for 2nd, Imperial livery lace on chest, sleeves and edging collar and turnbacks; green and yellow trumpet cords. Trumpeters did not wear the cuirass.

Cuirassiers

When Napoleon came to power, the French Army had 25 regiments of heavy cavalry whose tactical value was

Sub-Lieutenant Charles Le Grand, Provisional (later 13th) Cuirassiers, killed in Spain on 2 May 1808. Print after portrait by Baron Gros.

in doubt. In December 1802, the number was reduced to 18 and the 5th, 6th and 7th regiments were assigned to wear cuirasses. On 24 September 1803, the first 12 regiments were made cuirassiers and the rest converted into dragoons. With the cuirassier regiments, Napoleon now had the elite heavy shock cavalry he sought and he used them with considerable success. Each regiment had four squadrons each of two companies, each company having 100 men; five squadrons from March 1807; two provisional regiments created in 1808 to serve in Spain, become 13th regiment on 21 October 1808; 14th regiment created from Dutch cuirassiers on 24 December 1809; four squadrons per regiment from 18 January 1810; reduced to six regiment from August 1815.

Uniform: the cavalry regiments had blue coats with long tails until 1804 when all the regiments started wearing cuirasses and helmets. The helmets were of polished steel with brass comb, black mane, black cow

Opposite.
Trooper, 11th Cuirassiers, 1804. Print after Hoffman.

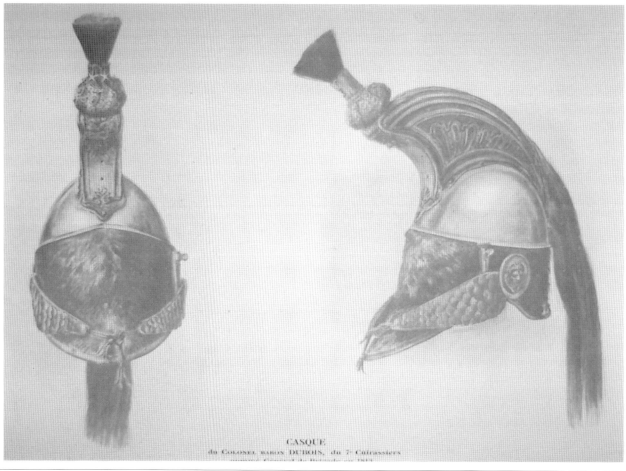

CASQUE
du COLONEL BARON DUBOIS, du 7ᵉ Cuirassiers

Opposite top.
Cuirassier helmet for enlisted men, c. 1804-1811. Part of the mane on the upper comb was tied up to form a sort of brush rising in front. Print after Raffet's sketches of helmets in museums.

Opposite bottom.
Helmet of Colonel Dubois, 7th Cuirassiers, c. 1812. Officer's helmets followed the same general design as the men but with refinements such as the lower part of the brush enclosed in brass and the fur turban also covering the visor. Print after Raffet.

hide turban, black visor edged with brass, red plume in a small brass socket on left side, brass chin scales. Senior officers had white plumes and gilded brass. The cuirass had front and back plates of polished steel, leather straps with brass scales, brass studs and fittings; the cuirass lining was red edged with white for all regiments. Armed with straight-bladed cavalry sword, carbine and, from 1806, pistols. A small black

Right.
Colonel Lataye, 10th Cuirassiers, c. 1810. Print after portrait.

Bottom.
Cuirass of Colonel Dubois, 7th Cuirassiers, c. 1812. Print after Raffet.

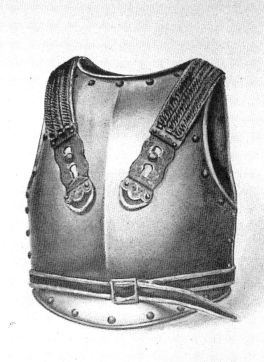

CUIRASSE
du COLONEL BARON DUBOIS, du 7ᵉ Cuirassiers (1812)
(D'APRÈS UNE AQUARELLE COMMUNIQUÉE PAR M. ÉDOUARD DETAILLE)

74 Heavy Cavalry

Trooper, 5th Cuirassiers, c. 1812-15, shown on a march. Note the helmet with the mane plaited, the plume covered by a cover, the grey overalls and the horse's tail tied up. Print after JOB.

Trumpeter, 6th Cuirassiers, 1808. Trumpeters had black sheepskin saddle covers edged orange for the 6th. Print after Martinet.

cartridge box on a white belt is worn over the cuirass, white sword belt at waist when mounted. Cuirassiers were mounted on blacks or dark bays.

The 24 September 1803 order only specified that the colour of the uniforms remained the same and 'only the changes in cut' for cuirassiers would be made, which meant a short-tailed coatee. The facings were to be scarlet collar, cuffs, lapels and turnbacks for the 1st to 6th regiments, yellow for 7th to 12th. However, it seems that the 3rd, 5th, 8th and 11th Cuirassiers had blue collars. In principle, the coatees had lapels but it seems some were in fact single-

Opposite.
Helmet and cuirass, 4th Cuirassiers, 1811-1815. In 1811, a new, much cheaper, pattern of helmet was introduced lacking the fluted embossing on the comb and without the brass rim edging the visor. It was not popular and the men kept wearing the old helmets whenever they could but several regiments only had them. Very few are now known to exist. Adrian Forman, Minehead, UK.

breasted. All had pewter buttons, silver for officers.

As for the cut of the coat, some regiments had them made with short tails. Inspection reports indicate that the 3rd, 7th, 9th and 10th had coatees by 1805 and the 2nd, 11th and 12th had them in late 1805 or early 1806. However, the 1st, 4th, 5th, 6th and 8th kept wearing long tailed coats as late as 1810-1811. Turnbacks had blue grenades. The blue shoulder straps piped with the facing colour were gradually replaced by red epaulettes.

The rest of the uniform consisted of: white waistcoat; buff breeches; long black boots with bronzed steel spurs; white gauntlet gloves; black cravat; white cloak; blue housings laced white, white sheepskin edged red, white grenades on the housings and regimental numbers on valise. On foot: blue surtout; white stockings, blue in winter; buckled shoes; bicorn with pompon. Stable dress: blue forage cap with blue turnup edged with white lace, piping of facing colour; blue stable jacket; white duck or linen pantaloons; wooden shoes.

Cuirassiers, like other elite troops, were proud of

Dragoons in campaign dress, c. 1800-1812. Print after Meissonnier.

Chef d'escadron Patenotre, 7th Dragoons, c. 1805-1812. Print after portrait.

their queues and seem to have abandoned them reluctantly; the 3rd Regiment still had them in 1809. Sideburns were to be no lower than the upper lip level and mustaches were compulsory from March to December.

The 13th regiment was assigned wine red ('lie-de-vin') facings. Initially, it seems to have used brown Spanish cloth for surtouts and brown pantaloons with red piping.

The 14th kept wearing its former Dutch uniform: steel helmet and cuirass (with medium blue lining edged yellow) as French cuirassiers, 'white coat, medium blue turnbacks, lapels to the waist, yellow [brass] buttons, red epaulettes, medium blue waistcoat with pockets, black cravat, white pantaloons, yellow gauntlet gloves and belts, white cloak.' In 1811, following the Emperor's suggestion, it adopted the blue French uniform with wine red facings and pewter buttons.

New facing colours were ordered for the 4th-6th and 10th-12th regiments, apparently in the later part of 1810 on a new 'coat-surtout' introduced at that time. It had round cuffs, no lapels and its tails were

fairly long going down to just above the back of the knee. The collar and cuffs were, depending on the regiment, of the facing colour piped blue or blue piped in the facing colour. The turnbacks were always of the facing colour with a blue grenade and the front was piped in the facing colour. The regimental facings were:

1st: scarlet cuffs and collar
2nd: scarlet cuffs, blue collar
3rd: blue cuffs, scarlet collar
4th: orange cuffs and collar
5th: orange cuffs, blue collar
6th: blue cuffs, orange collar
7th: yellow cuffs and collar
8th: yellow cuffs, blue collar
9th: blue cuffs, yellow collar
10th: pink cuffs and collar

Opposite.
Brigadier, 4th Dragoons, c. 1808, 'leaving the cantonment' with some obvious regrets. Print after Martinet. Anne S.K. Brown Military Collection, Brown University, USA.

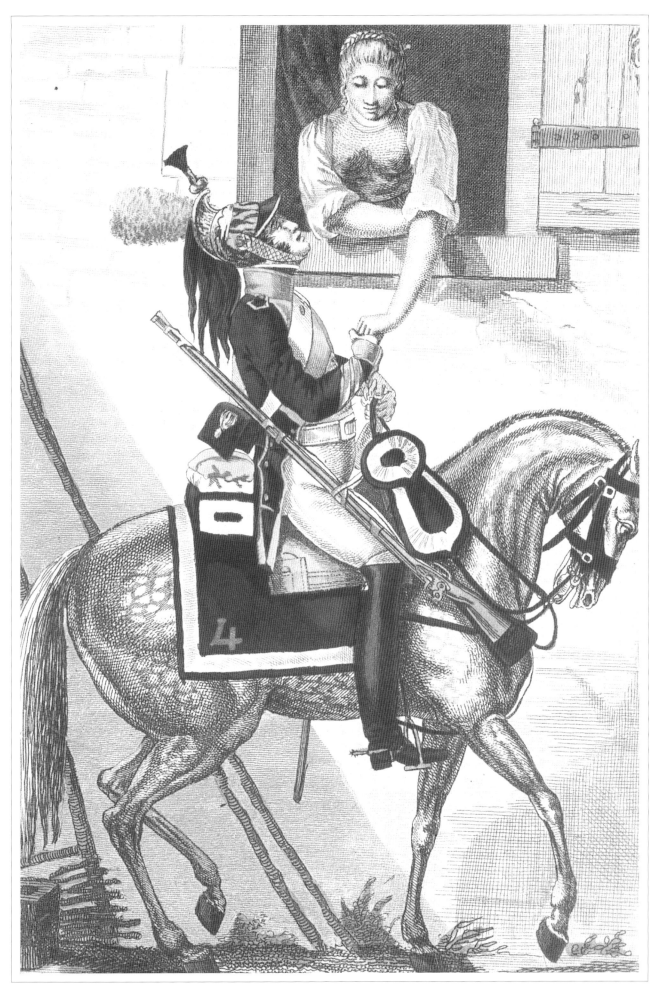

Band of the 4th Dragoons, early 1800s. Painting by Édouard Détaille. Mr. & Mrs. Don Troiani, Southbury, CT.

11th: pink cuffs, blue collar
12th: blue cuffs, pink collar
13th: wine red cuffs and collar
14th: wine red cuffs, blue collar

The orders of 7 February 1812 brought substantial changes to the uniforms of cuirassiers. All were now officially to have a single-breasted coatee with nine pewter button and red epaulettes. The collar, turnbacks (which had a blue grenade) and piping were always of the facings colours but cuffs and cuff flaps otherwise varied for each regiment as follows:

1st: red cuffs and cuff flaps
2nd: red and cuffs, blue cuff flaps
3rd: blue cuffs, red cuff flaps
4th: orange cuffs and cuff flaps
5th: orange cuffs, blue cuff flaps
6th: blue cuffs, orange cuff flaps
7th: yellow cuffs and cuff flaps
8th: yellow cuffs, blue cuff flaps
9th: blue cuffs, yellow cuff flaps
10th: pink cuffs and cuff flaps

11th: pink cuffs, blue cuff flaps
12th: blue cuffs, pink cuff flaps
13th: wine red cuffs and cuff flaps
14th: wine red cuffs, blue cuff flaps

Other novelties included grey overalls and white cloak flecked with blue. Other items as before. There were no further major changes in the uniform.

Trumpeters, from 1804: helmet with red or white mane; single-breasted coatee either of the facing colour or blue with cuffs and collar edged with silver or white lace, white lace at buttonholes on the front. For instance, before 1810, the 1st and 4th's trumpeters had: white helmet mane, red plume; red coatee, red edged silver collar and cuffs, white turnbacks with red grenades, seven white laces on the chest, white epaulettes. The 6th had, in c. 1810-12, white mane and red plume; blue coatee with orange edged silver collar and cuffs, red epaulettes with white crescent, orange laces on chest. The 7th had a yellow coatee, the 8th an orange coatee. The 13th had, in 1812, a white mane, wine red coatee with five white laces in

Opposite.

Trumpeter, elite company, 21st Dragoons, 1802-1812. Print after JOB.

front. From 1812, the cuirassiers trumpeters adopted the green imperial livery coatee with collar, cuffs and turnbacks of the facing colour, imperial livery lace. They did not wear the cuirass and were mounted on whites or greys.

Dragoons

When the Revolution broke out in 1789, there were 18 dragoon regiments in the army. In 1793, three more were added, each regiment having four squadrons, each squadron having two companies of 100 men each. In September 1803, several heavy cavalry and hussar regiments were converted to dragoons forming the 22nd to the 30th regiments; 1805, four temporary regiments of foot dragoons formed with detachments, two temporary regiments in 1806; 1807, each company to have 128 men including four officers; 1808, eight sappers created per regiment; in 1811, the 1st, 8th, 9th, 10th and 29th regiments are converted into Chevau-légers-lanciers regiment; further reduced to 15 regiments in May 1814.

Uniform: green coat with lapels and turnbacks of the regimental facing colour and the collar, cuffs, cuff flaps and piping edging the facings either of the facing colour or green depending on the regiment, vertical or horizontal pockets depending on the regiment (see regimental distinctions below), green shoulder straps piped with facing colour but many regiments had white epaulettes instead, green grenades on turnbacks; pewter buttons; white waistcoat and breeches; black long boots; brass helmet with brass crest, black mane, sealskin turban, black leather visor, plume varied considerably (see below), brass chin scales; bearskin cap with red plume, red or white cords, red back panel with white cross, red epaulettes for élite companies; green surtout and green stable jacket, sometimes with collar of the regimental facing colour; green forage cap with piping of the facing colour, white lace and grenade; white duck trousers; grey overalls with buttons on side; white gauntlet gloves; off-white cloak; green housings edged white with white number, also white sheepskin edged with facing colour. Sappers had bearskin caps with red cords, plumes and back panel with white cross; red epaulettes, red crossed axes on upper sleeves; white or buff apron.

From February 1812, coatee in the same colours; plumes no longer issued for helmets, only pompons which were red, sky blue, orange and violet for the first company of each squadron, same colours with a white centre for the second companies. Armed with a dragoon musket with bayonet and sword. Officers: silver buttons and lace; the brass on their helmet was guilded, turban of leopard fur (usually imitation) often

going over the visor, white plumes for senior officers

Foot Dragoons, 1805-06: had the same uniform as the units they were detached from except for infantry gaiters, shoes, knapsack. In 1805, the 1st regiment was made up of detachments from the 1st, 2nd, 4th, 14th, 20th and 26th; 2nd regiment from the 3rd, 6th, 10th, 11th, 13th and 22nd; 3rd regiment from the 5th, 8th, 9th, 12th, 16th and 21st; 4th regiment from the 15th, 17th, 18th, 19th, 25th and 27th. In 1806, the 1st regiment was from the 2nd, 6th, 11th, 13th, 14th, 20th, 22nd and 26th; the 2nd regiment from the 8th, 12th, 16th, 17th, 18th, 21st, 25th and 27th.

Trumpeters: reversed colours, facings sometimes edged with white lace, the coat often single breasted with white buttonholes in front, no cuff flaps, white epaulettes; white or red mane on helmet. Same dress for Foot Dragoons but brass drums with blue hoops instead of trumpets. Imperial livery from 1812. They rode whites or greys.

1st: scarlet lapels, collar, cuffs and cuff flaps, horizontal pockets; scarlet plume, also bottom half green with scarlet top half.

2nd: scarlet lapels and cuffs, green collar and cuff flaps, horizontal pockets; white epaulettes; plume bottom half green with scarlet top half, also all red.

3rd: scarlet lapels and collar, green cuffs, scarlet cuff flaps, horizontal pockets; red-white-red plume.

4th: scarlet lapels, collar, cuffs and cuff flaps, vertical pockets; white plume.

5th: scarlet lapels and cuffs, green collar and cuff flaps, vertical pockets; white plume.

6th: scarlet lapels and collar, green cuffs, scarlet cuff flaps, vertical pockets; plume bottom half green with scarlet top half.

7th: crimson lapels, collar, cuffs and cuff flaps, horizontal pockets; plume half red and half green.

8th: crimson lapels and cuffs, green collar and cuff flaps, horizontal pockets; white plume; plume half red and half green.

9th: crimson lapels and collar, green cuffs, crimson cuff flaps, horizontal pockets; white epaulettes; red plume.

10th: crimson lapels, collar, cuffs and cuff flaps, vertical pockets; crimson plume.

11th: crimson lapels and cuffs, green collar and cuff flaps, vertical pockets; white plume.

12th: crimson lapels and collar, green cuffs, crimson cuff flaps, vertical pockets; plume half red and half green, also half white and half red.

13th: dark pink lapels, collar, cuffs and cuff flaps, horizontal pockets; plume half red and half green.

14th: dark pink lapels and cuffs, green collar and cuff flaps, horizontal pockets

15th: dark pink lapels and collar, green cuffs, dark pink cuff flaps, horizontal pockets

16th: dark pink lapels, collar, cuffs and cuff flaps, vertical pockets; white plume.

17th: dark pink lapels and cuffs, green collar and cuff flaps, vertical pockets; white epaulettes; red, also white plume.

18th: dark pink lapels and collar, green cuffs, dark pink cuff flaps, vertical pockets; plume half white and half red. In 1808, the regiment received brown coats (faced dark pink) due to difficulties in obtaining green cloth.

19th: yellow lapels, collar, cuffs and cuff flaps, horizontal pockets; white epaulettes; white plume, also bottom half green with yellow top half.

20th: yellow lapels and cuffs, green collar and cuff flaps, horizontal pockets; plume bottom half green with yellow top half, also half yellow and half white.

21st: yellow lapels and collar, green cuffs, yellow cuff flaps, horizontal pockets; white plume.

22nd: yellow lapels, collar, cuffs and cuff flaps, vertical pockets; white epaulettes; red plume, also half black and half yellow.

23rd: yellow lapels and cuffs, green collar and cuff flaps, vertical pockets; white plume.

24th: yellow lapels and collar, green cuffs, yellow cuff flaps, vertical pockets; white plume, also half white and half yellow.

25th: orange lapels, collar, cuffs and cuff flaps, horizontal pockets; red epaulettes having green straps with two white line; plume bottom half green with orange top half.

26th: orange lapels and cuffs, green collar and cuff flaps, horizontal pockets

27th: orange lapels and collar, green cuffs, orange cuff flaps, horizontal pockets; brass chains on each shoulder.

28th: orange lapels, collar, cuffs and cuff flaps, vertical pockets; white plume.

29th: orange lapels and cuffs, green collar and cuff flaps, vertical pockets; white plume.

30th: orange lapels and collar, green cuffs, orange

Trumpeter of elite company, 23rd Dragoons, c. 1800-1812. Print after Édouard Détaille.

cuff flaps, vertical pockets; red plume.

Guides Interprètes de l'Armée d'Allemagne

Guides Interpreters of the Army of Germany. Two squadrons created in October 1805, recruited among German speaking dragoons to serve as interpreters and messengers. Disbanded 30 June 1807, the men were incorporated into Marshal Berthier's Guides.

Uniform: completely white surtout, yellow aiguillette; brass buttons; white waistcoat; white-buff breeches; brass dragoon helmet; white housings and sheepskin edged yellow.

82 Light Cavalry

Light Cavalry

The largest body of cavalry in Napoleon's army was the light horse which amounted to nearly fifty regiments of hussars and Chasseurs à cheval by 1814. There was no real difference between the chasseurs and hussars, both performed the same tactical duties and were, in their day, among the best light cavalry in Europe.

Hussars

The first six hussar regiments were from the old royal army and numbered from 1791; another seven regiments were raised from various volunteers made into permanent units from 1792 to 1795; 13th Hussars disbanded in 1796; on 24 September 1803, the 7th bis, 11th and 12th Hussars converted into dragoons; new 11th formed 25 December 1810; 9th bis formed in Spain from 10 January 1812; 12th, 13th and 14th formed in 1813 and new 14th in 1814 (see details below); reduced to six regiments from May 1814. Hussar regiments generally had four squadrons each of two companies, each company of 128 each, the total establishment being, from 1807, of 1000 NCOs and hussars led by 43 officers. Each regiment had an elite company being the 1st company.

Hussar regiments had many peculiarities in organization and uniforms far too numerous to relate here. Insofar as the uniforms are concerned, the details given bellow hold for the period going from 1803 to 1815. While general features remain before that time frame, many aspects such as headgear varied a great deal from one unit to another and even within the same regiment. With plumes notably, the variations seem endless during the Imperial era. What is given here is what seems to have been the general trend in a

unit but certainly not the affirmation it was its only practice. In matters of uniforms, hussars were reputed, and rightly so, to be the most outlandish dressers in the army – the proudly self-avowed 'black sheeps' of the military bureaucrats at HQ trying to regulate their dress and hair styles.

Uniforms: the hussar had a dress of central European origin, Hungarian in particular, which came to France with the first units of mercenary hussars at the end of the 17th century. These corps soon were increasingly recruited with Frenchmen who appreciated the dashing style as well as the novel light cavalry tactics. By the time of the French Revolution, there were many aspiring 'beau sabreurs' which eventually formed the backbone of some of the finest hussar units on record during the Empire.

Hussars wore a short jacket called a dolman, an over jacket trimmed with fur called a pelisse slung with studied 'negligence' over the left shoulder when not worn, a sash with small 'barrels' and knots, tight breeches and boots. The dolman, pelisse and breeches were elaborately decorated with about 18 cord loops tied to, generally, five rows of small ball buttons on the front, the breeches being also much braided. Hanging on three slings from their waistbelt was a sabretache, a flat leather case with a decorated flap meant to carry dispatches but admittedly more useful for love notes to woo local girls.

Early hussar shakos had a 'wing' wrapped around them but this feature seem to have gone out of use by about 1806. Unless otherwise noted, the shakos were black, wider at the top than bottom, with cords of the regimental colour, chin scales and shako plates added from about 1805-1806. The plumes and cords were officially abolished in November 1811 but many continued to wear them even with the black waxed cloth shako covers. From 1812, cylindrical shakos with no plates but a cockade held by a loop in front started replacing the previous type.

The whole business of hair styles was a moot point

Opposite.

4th Hussars, c. 1800-1805. Officer in the foreground with enlisted hussars on a patrol wearing their pelisses in cool mountainous country. Painting by Édouard Détaille. Mr. & Mrs. Don Troiani, Southbury, CT.

Chef d'escadron Du Pouget, 5th Hussars, at the siege of Wesel, 1813. Print after contemporary. painting.

Trumpeter's dolman, 4th Hussars, c. 1805-1810. Back view. Formerly in the M.H. de Young Museum, San Francisco.

with hussars. Part of their claim to fame was the wearing of not only queues, but also of 'cadenettes' which were pleated lengths of hair coming down on the side of each cheek, and, of course moustaches. While the moustaches remained, the queues and pleats were ordered to be cut in 1805. Naturally, the hussars resisted but, in time, the regiments obeyed finding the Neo-Roman 'Titus' style to be quite acceptable and less trouble. But some held out and the 5th Hussars was probably the last to have queues. 'Many times,' recalled d'Espinchal of the 5th, 'the colonel, on the verge of ordering the execution of the order, had ceded to the troop's grief [at having to cut them]; but an ultimate order from the minister of war permitted no further delays...' This was at the beginning of 1808 (!) and the order was finally executed swiftly, each hussar being ordered to cut the queues of the next man in file. Within a few minutes 'eight hundred queues were left on the field' which the regiment immediately left, without leaving the hussars a chance to bid 'adieu' to an ornament so dear to them. By that evening, they had forgotten about queues and the 'Titus' hair style was now that of the regiment.

Hussars also had undress and ordinary campaign garments. This consisted of a forage cap, a stable jacket and a pair of overalls which buttoned on the outside and often strapped with black leather. Units in Spain often used the local brown cloth for repairs and replacements of undress items, and this of course made wags in the 2nd Hussars boast that all hussars wished to adopt their uniform!

The uniforms of the hussar regiments from c. 1803 to 1815 were generally as follows:

1st: sky blue dolman and dolman collar, red dolman cuffs; sky blue pelisse edged with black fur; sky blue breeches; pewter buttons; white cords; red and white sash; sky blue pantaloons with red stripe; black shako plume; sky blue stable jacket, red cuffs, white piping edging collar and cuffs; all sky blue forage cap

Opposite.
Trumpeter's dolman, 4th Hussars, c. 1805-1810. Front view. Red with blue collar and cuffs, brass ball buttons, yellow cords and lace. A superb example of a rare garment. Formerly in the M.H. de Young Museum, San Francisco.

Auguste Fesquet, officer, 5th Hussars, c. 1807. Print after miniature.

Captain Bro de Commère, 7th Hussars, 1810. Print after a miniature signed Jacques.

piped white, white lace edging turnup. Elite company black bearskin busby with red plume and red bag piped white. From late 1813, black cylindrical shako. Silver buttons, cords and lace for officers. Trumpeters: red dolman and dolman collar, sky blue cuffs; red pelisse with black fur; sky blue breeches; pewter buttons; white cords; red trumpet cords; sky blue sabretache laced red and piped white; black sheepskin housings edged scarlet.

2nd: brown dolman and dolman collar, sky blue dolman cuffs; brown pelisse edged with black fur; sky blue breeches; pewter buttons; white cords; red and white sash; sky blue pantaloons with brown stripe; black shako plume; brown stable jacket, sky blue cuffs, white piping edging collar and cuffs; brown forage cap piped white, white lace edging sky blue turnup. Elite company black bearskin busby with red plume and sky blue bag piped white. From late 1813, black cylindrical shako. Silver buttons, cords and lace for officers. Trumpeters: sky blue dolman and dolman collar, brown cuffs; sky blue pelisse; red trumpet cords; red sabretache laced white with gold eagle; brown pantaloons with white stripe.

3rd: grey dolman and dolman collar, red dolman cuffs; grey pelisse edged with black fur; grey breeches; pewter buttons; red cords; red and white sash; grey pantaloons with no stripe; black shako plume; grey stable jacket, red cuffs; all grey forage cap piped red, red lace edging turnup. Elite company black bearskin busby with red plume and red bag piped crimson. From late 1813, black cylindrical shako. Silver buttons, cords and lace for officers. Trumpeters: same as regiment but red breeches, black fur busby with red bag and plume.

4th: blue dolman and dolman collar (sometimes shown red), red dolman cuffs; red pelisse edged with black fur; blue breeches; brass buttons; yellow cords; red and yellow sash; blue pantaloons with red stripe; black shako plume; blue stable jacket, red cuffs; red forage cap piped yellow, yellow lace edging blue turnup. Elite company in Spain had black bearskin busby with brass grenade, red plume and red bag piped yellow, mounted on black horses with black

Opposite.

Trumpeter, 11th Hussars, 1810. Print after Édouard Détaille.

1st Lancer Regiment of the Vistula Legion and 2nd Hussars, Albuera (Spain), 16 May 1811.

This plate shows one of the most epic incidents of the Peninsular War, occurring during the battle of Albuera, pitting General Beresford's British, Spanish and Portuguese troops against Marshal Soult's French army which was slowly withdrawing from Portugal into Spain. At one point in the struggle, as a rain and hail storm broke over an already bloody battlefield, Brigadier General Sir John Colborne's brigade consisting of the 3rd (The Buffs), 31st, 48th and 66th regiments of foot seemed to be gaining the advantage. But as they advanced, their flank and rear became vulnerable. French cavalry commander and first rate tactician General Latour-Maubourg perceived Colborne's weakness. He immediately ordered the charge of two battle-hardened light cavalry regiments, the 1st Lancers of the Polish Vistula Legion and the 2nd French Hussar Regiment.

In some confusion at the novel sight of lancers, the British brigade faced about to meet the coming onslaught but it was in vain. In a flash, the lancers and hussars were upon them and, with irresistible élan, swept all over the redcoats in a terrible carnage by lance spearings and sabre cuts. Within a few minutes, the 3rd Buffs, the 48th and 66th were destroyed, half killed or wounded and the rest prisoners. The lancers then overwhelmed the gunners of a nearby British battery and captured its guns. The charge was so quick and fierce that even General Beresford barely escaped from a Polish lancer. Only the 31st managed to hold on until more British and Spanish units came up.

Albuera ended as something of a draw with awesome casualties to both armies. Soult finally withdrew his forces so that the British claimed victory but the sabre flashing, brown and sky blue hussars, and especially the lance wielding Poles clad in blue and yellow impressed so deeply the British that they eventually created their own lancer regiments. Painting by Christa Hook.

Top.
Officers, 3rd Hussars, 1813. Print after contemporary painting.

with black plume tipped red and red bag piped white. From 1812, red cylindrical shako. Silver buttons, cords and lace for officers. Trumpeters: red dolman, green collar and cuffs; red pelisse.

9th: red dolman, sky blue collar and cuffs; sky blue pelisse edged with black fur; sky blue breeches; brass buttons; yellow cords; red and yellow sash; sky blue pantaloons with red stripe; black shako plume with white tip; all sky blue stable jacket, yellow piping edging collar and cuffs; all sky blue forage cap piped yellow, yellow lace edging turnup. Elite company black bearskin busby with red plume and red bag piped yellow. From late 1813, red cylindrical shako. Gold buttons, cords and lace for officers. Trumpeters: yellow dolman, red collar and cuffs; scarlet pelisse; scarlet breeches; brass buttons; black cords; crimson and black sash; boots edged orange; red sabretache laced orange with brass eagle and green laurels; green trumpet cords; sky blue shako with orange lace and cords, yellow plume. Also, yellow pelisse with black cords; sky blue breeches with yellow cords; elite company trumpeters had black busby with yellow bag, yellow plume with black base; black sheepskin housings edged red.

9th bis (formed January 1812, incorporated into 12th in January 1813): red dolman, red dolman collar and cuffs; sky blue dolman edged with black fur; sky blue breeches; pewter buttons; white cords. Silver buttons, cords and lace for officers.

10th: sky blue dolman, red collar and cuffs; sky

blue pelisse edged with black fur; sky blue breeches; pewter buttons; white cords; red and white sash; sky blue pantaloons with red stripe; black shako plume with red lower third; sky blue stable jacket, red cuffs and collar; all sky blue forage cap piped white, white lace edging turnup. Elite company black bearskin busby with red plume and red bag piped white with white tassel. Silver buttons, cords and lace for officers. Trumpeters: red dolman, sky blue dolman collar and cuffs; red pelisse; blue trumpet cords; busby with yellow bag piped white; red valise edged white.

11th (converted into 29th Dragoons on 24 September 1803): light green dolman, light blue-grey collar and cuffs; light green pelisse edged with black fur; light blue-grey breeches; pewter buttons; white cords; crimson and white sash; red waistcoat; black shako with light blue-grey edged black wing.

11th (formed December 1810 with 2nd Dutch Hussars): blue dolman, red collar and cuffs; blue pelisse edged with white fur; blue breeches; brass buttons; yellow cords; red and white sash, blue line in centre of white; blue pantaloons with narrow red stripe; black shako plume; stable jacket, red cuffs, white piping edging collar and cuffs; all blue forage cap piped yellow, yellow lace edging turnup. Elite company white busby with red plume and red bag piped yellow. From 1812, black cylindrical shako. Gold buttons, cords and lace for officers. Trumpeters: white dolman, blue collar and cuffs; white pelisse; blue breeches; yellow and blue cords; black busby.

12th (converted into 30th Dragoons on 24 September 1803): brown dolman, sky blue collar and cuffs; sky blue pelisse edged with black fur; sky blue breeches; pewter buttons; white cords; crimson and white sash; sky blue waistcoat; black shako with sky blue edged white wing.

12th (formed January 1813 with remnants of 9th bis): red dolman, sky blue collar and cuffs; sky blue pelisse edged with black fur; sky blue breeches; pewter buttons; white cords; red and white sash; black shako plume with yellow tip. Green cloak, stable jacket and trousers. Elite company black bearskin busby with red plume and red bag piped white with white tassel. Silver buttons, cords and lace for officers. Trumpeters: white dolman, sky blue collar and cuffs; white pelisse edged with brown fur; red cords on dolman and pelisse.

13th or 'Bacciochi's' Hussars created 28 January 1813, raised in Italy, incorporated into 14th on 13 December 1813: brown dolman, sky blue collar and cuffs; brown pelisse edged with black fur; sky blue breeches; pewter buttons; white cords; red and white sash; sky blue pantaloons with brown stripe; black

Colonel Méda, 1st Chasseurs à cheval, c. 1807-1812. Print after portrait.

Colonel Shée, 13th Chasseurs à cheval, c. 1812-1814. Print after miniature.

shako, green plume tipped red. Elite company black bearskin busby with red plume and sky blue bag piped white with white tassel, also black shako with red bands. Silver buttons, cords and lace for officers. Trumpeters: brown dolman, green collar and cuffs; brown pelisse; green breeches; pewter buttons; white cords; black busby, green bag, black plume; sheepskin housingsedged red.

13th or 'Jérome Napoléon' Hussars created 31 July 1813, raised in Westphalia, reorganized 1 January 1814 and numbered 13th Hussars, remnants dissolved late March 1814: red dolman and collar, sky blue cuffs; sky blue pelisse edged with white fur; sky blue breeches; brass buttons; yellow cords; red, white and blue sash; red shako with yellow top band, black lower band, brass plate with JN cipher (later 13), yellow cords, white plume. Gold cords and lace for officers. Trumpeters: white dolman, sky blue collar and cuffs; white pelisse edged with black fur; brass buttons; yellow cords; red breeches; shako same as men but blue tip on white plume. Imperial livery may have been worn in 1814.

14th (formed January 1813 from various

nationalities, eventually partly deserted to allies): brown dolman, sky blue collar and cuffs; brown pelisse edged with black fur; sky blue breeches; pewter buttons; white cords; red and white sash; sky blue pantaloons with brown stripe; black cylindrical shako. Silver buttons, cords and lace for officers. Trumpeters: brown dolman, sky blue collar and cuffs; brown pelisse; sky blue breeches with green cords; pewter buttons; white cords; black busby, sky blue bag, black plume

14th (formed January 1814 with remnants of 13th and 14th): green dolman, red dolman collar and cuffs; green pelisse edged with black fur; red breeches; pewter buttons; red cords with black thread; red and green sash; red cylindrical shako. Silver buttons, cords and lace for officers.

Chasseurs à Cheval

There were 12 Chasseurs à cheval (Mounted Chasseurs) light cavalry regiments at the time of the French Revolution. It was a relatively new arm which, in 1793, leapt to 23 regiments by the incorporation of various independent volunteer units although the 17th

Elite Company of the 5th Chasseurs à cheval, c. 1805. Print after H. Chartier.

and 18th regiments were disbanded the following year and their numbers remained vacant until 1811. The 24th, 25th and 26th regiments were raised in 1801. The 27th was formed in September 1806, the 28th in May 1808, the 29th in August 1809, the 30th in December 1810. In 1811, the vacant 17th and 18th regiments were ordered re-raised and the 31st created. From 1796, each regiment had 941 men including 38 officers in four squadrons. In March 1807, the organization was ordered to be the same as hussar regiments. In May 1814, the number of regiments was reduced to 15.

Uniform: the dress of the Chasseurs à cheval varied greatly during the Napoleonic era. They initially had a hussar-style dress featuring a green dolman with white metal buttons and white cords, cuffs and collar colours depending on the regiment. The dolman was worn until about 1805-06 (later for some units) when replaced by a green coat with green lapels piped with the facing colour. A green surtout was often worn for undress. In 1808-09, the green 'à la Kinski' coatee, which was single breasted, appeared. A green coatee with green lapels also appeared in some regiments at

the same time. It was replaced in 1813 by the 1812 green regulation coatee which had green lapels. All these garments had piping and turnbacks of the facing colour. Buttons were of white metal for all.

The Chasseurs à cheval wore a waistcoat which could be red, white, green or of the facing colour, often braided hussar-style with white cords. Green hussar breeches with white braid, hussar boots, green overalls with stripe of the facing colour. Initially, the shako with a wing wrapped around it, of the facing colour, was worn until about 1805-06, replaced by the ordinary black shako with a cockade and loop in front, with a plume and later a pompon of the company colour (sky blue, yellow, orange, violet) and white cords. Elite companies usually had a busby with bag of the facing colour piped white and a red plume, white cords and often red epaulettes.

Trumpeters generally, but not always, wore reversed colours to 1813 when nearly all took the green imperial livery coatee trimmed with livery lace. Housings were of white sheepskin edged with facing colour, valises green with white lace.

In spite of a certain apparent uniformity because all wore green, the Chasseurs à cheval had, perhaps, the most varied dress of the all arms of service. The main features only, for this is hardly exhaustive, for each

Chef d'escadron Raveneau, 14th Chasseurs à cheval, c. 1805.
Print after portrait.

regiment are given below:

1st: scarlet collar and cuffs. Dolman to about 1807; coatee with lapels until 1813, M. 1812 coatee thereafter. Scarlet vest with white cords. Red leather belts for officers. Shako with scarlet wing, green plume tipped scarlet; leather helmet with brass fittings, black crest and white plume in 1815. Trumpeters: reversed colours, from 1809 white buttonhole lace on lapels and red vest with white cords; busby with green tipped red plume; Imperial livery from 1813.

2nd: green collar, scarlet cuffs. Dolman to about 1807; Kinski coatee with white waistcoat 1808-12; from 1813, M. 1812 coatee. Red waistcoat for elite company. Trumpeters: reversed colours, imperial livery from 1813.

3rd: scarlet collar and cuffs for dolman to about 1808 then coat with lapels and coatee with lapels from c. 1809, M. 1812 coatee with scarlet collar and green cuffs from 1813. White waistcoat. Red plume tipped green. Elite company officers had pelisses. Trumpeters: sky blue coatee with scarlet regimental facings, scarlet shako with black top and bottom bands

and green plume, red overalls; Imperial livery from 1813.

4th: yellow collar and cuffs. Dolman to 1808, also coatee with lapels from 1802; Kinski coatee from 1809-13, M. 1812 coatee thereafter. Shako with yellow wing, green plume with yellow tip. Grey overalls piped yellow. Trumpeters: reversed colours, imperial livery from 1813.

5th: green collar, yellow cuffs. Dolman to 1808, cords mixed yellow and green in 1807-08; coatee with lapels from 1809, M. 1812 coatee from 1813. Green pelisse to about 1806. Shako with green wing, changed yellow c. 1802, black plume with yellow tip. Yellow belts. Green overalls with yellow stripes. Trumpeters: blue coat to about 1800, regimental reversed colours with green cords; appears to have worn a yellow Kinski coatee with imperial livery lace from 1813.

6th: yellow collar, green cuffs. Dolman to 1806; also coat to 1809 then coatee with lapels, M. 1812 coatee from 1813. White waistcoat. Shako with yellow wing, plume black with yellow lower third. Leather helmet with brass plate and black crest in 1815. Trumpeters: red with yellow collar and cuffs, white lace, yellow czapska with green plume in 1809, afterwards white coatee with yellow collar, cuffs and lapels. In 1814, yellow coatee, green collar and cuffs, red buttonholes on chest, white epaulettes (red for elite), yellow shako with red band and black plume.

7th: pink collar and cuffs. Dolman to 1806; also coat to 1809, Kinski coatee to 1813, M. 1812 coatee thereafter. Red waistcoat, white in summer. Shako with pink wing, various plumes including red-white-blue and red with black bottom and later black with pink top. Trumpeters: green coat with white lace then blue from about 1805, pink faced green from 1808, pink shako with white lace or busby with pink bag; imperial green livery from 1814.

8th: green dolman with pink collar and cuffs to about 1804, then green coat, from 1809 the coatee with lapels and green collar and pink cuffs, M. 1812 coatee from 1813. Trumpeters: in 1806-07, pink coatee faced green with white lace and epaulettes, green vest with pink cords; imperial livery from 1813.

9th: pink collar, green cuffs. Dolman to about 1805; also coatee with lapels to 1809, Kinski coatee to 1813, M. 1812 coatee thereafter. White waistcoat. Green plume with bottom third pink, later green tipped pink. Trumpeters: as for 8th regiment.

Opposite.

Trooper, 19th Chasseurs à cheval, 1808. This unit wore the dolman until about 1810. Print after Martinet. Anne S.K. Brown Military Collection, Brown University, USA.

Officer, 3rd Chevau-Légers-Lanciers, c. 1811-1812. Print after Martinet. Anne S.K. Brown Military Collection, Brown University, USA.

13th: orange collar and cuffs. Dolman to about 1807, also coat with lapels, coatee with lapels from 1809 to 1813 then M. 1812 coatee. Green over orange plume, later green plume tipped orange. Trumpeters: reversed colours, imperial livery from 1813.

14th: dolman with orange collar and cuffs to about 1805, coat with green collar and orange cuffs to 1808 then Kinski coatee to 1813 when M. 1812 coatee is taken. White waistcoat or orange with white cords. Green over orange plume. Trumpeters: reversed colours, seems not to have adopted the Imperial livery.

15th: dolman with orange collar and cuffs to about 1804, coat with orange collar and green cuffs to 1809, then Kinski coatee, M. 1812 from 1813. Green waistcoat with white cords. Red hussar style breeches in full dress, brown overalls with leather inset in Spain. The men of this regiment still had queues in 1813. Trumpeters: reversed colours, red breeches to 1810, sky blue faced orange to 1813 then the imperial livery.

16th: sky blue collar and cuffs. Dolman to about 1806, coat to about 1809 then Kinski coatee to 1813 when M. 1812 coatee is adopted. White waistcoat. Sky blue over green plume, later green with sky blue lower third. Trumpeters: reversed colours coatee without lapels but with wide buttonholes on chest, sky blue shako with white plume tipped sky blue; in 1812 sky blue Kinski jacket, white epaulettes, green overalls with false boots and sky blue stripes, light blue czapska; imperial livery from 1813.

17th (ordered re-raised in 1811 but not actually formed): was to have green collar, sky blue cuffs. Green plume tipped sky blue.

18th (ordered re-raised in 1811 but not actually formed): was to have sky blue collar, green cuffs. Sky blue plume with green lower third.

19th: orange collar and cuffs. Dolman to about 1810, coat also worn, coatee with lapels from 1810, green overalls with white stripe, M. 1812 coatee from 1813. Shako with orange wing edged white. Trumpeters: reversed colours, imperial livery from 1813.

20th: dolman with orange collar and cuffs to about 1805, also coat with green collar (from c. 1805), orange cuffs to about 1810-11 then Kinski coatee, M. 1812 coatee from 1813. The men had queues until 1813. Officers and NCOs in Spain had orange breeches. Trumpeters: reversed colours, Imperial livery not adopted. Commander Parquin of the 20th, who joined his regiment as a volunteer in January 1803, left us an exceptional description of his regiment. His unit then wore 'a black shako, of an elegant shape, surmounted by an aurore [orange] flame ending in a point. This flame left floating with

10th: crimson collar and cuffs. Dolman to about 1808; also coat with lapels, from 1809 coatee with lapels, M. 1812 coatee from 1813. White waistcoat. Crimson over black plume. Trumpeters: crimson dolman faced green with white cords to about 1808, then crimson faced red coatee with white lace; imperial livery from 1813.

11th: dolman with crimson collar and cuffs to about 1805; also coat with lapels to 1813, M. 1812 coatee with green collar and crimson cuffs thereafter. White waistcoat. Crimson over black plume. Trumpeters: coat of reversed colours with white lace at collar and cuffs in c. 1809; imperial livery from 1813.

12th: dolman with crimson collar and cuffs to 1804, coat to 1809, coatee with lapels with crimson collar and green cuffs, M. 1812 from 1813. White waistcoat. Shako with crimson wing. Green plume tipped red, black plume tipped crimson from 1809. Officers had a summer dress of pale yellow cotton dolman faced crimson with crimson pantaloons all with silver cords. Trumpeters: sky blue faced crimson in 1804, crimson coatee faced green from 1809; Imperial livery from 1813.

the red and black plume announced the full dress. We wore the queue four inches [long] from the hair, one inch covered with black ribbon and one inch [flowing] below the queue. Two sturdy and long braids hung at the cheeks and ended with a small piece of ribbon lead. The hair and braids were greased and powdered. Green dolman, orange cuffs and piping, white wool cords, five rows of ball buttons, Hungarian [style] breeches with wool cords; hussar boots; green and orange sash, eight inches wide with tassels of the same colour. Finally, gauntlet gloves completed this brilliant uniform. Each chasseur had a sabretache hanging about two feet [from the waist] on the left side and held by three straps from sabre belt. This sabretache was used to carry letters when the chasseurs were on dispatch service, and for their handkerchief if they had one.' In 1805, Parquin noted that 'after leaving Breda, the regiment received the order to cut the queues and the braids, which left us in despair. It took no less than the all-powerful reasoning of the officers, who told the troopers that, as we were going on campaign, it would be much cleaner and better at war.'

21st: dolman with red-orange collar and cuffs to about 1803-05, coat with red-orange collar and green cuffs then coatee with lapels from 1809, M. 1812 coatee from 1813. Red-orange waistcoat with white cords. Green plume with orange base. Trumpeters: reversed colours, white lace and epaulettes, red waistcoat with white cords, green breeches, red-orange czapska.

22nd: red-orange collar and cuffs. Dolman to about 1803, coat to 1809, coatee with lapels to 1813 then M. 1812 coatee. Red waistcoat. Red-orange over green plume. Trumpeters: reversed colours, Imperial livery from 1813.

23rd: dolman with red-orange collar and cuffs to about 1803, coat with green collar and red-orange cuffs to about 1810 then Kinski coatee, M. 1812 coatee from 1813. Officers often had red-orange breeches up to about 1806, red-orange overalls for officers and NCOs around 1811, green or grey overalls with red-orange stripes for troopers. White waistcoat. According to Colonel Marbot, during 1813, much of the regiment sported white pelisses with 'gold' cords captured from Austrian hussars. In early 1814, the regiment was armed with lances. Trumpeters: in 1811, red (red-orange?) Kinski coatee with yellow cuffs, turnbacks and star on collar, white lace on chest, yellow shako with white band and plume; imperial livery from 1813.

24th: dolman with yellow collar and scarlet cuffs to about 1805, coat with red-orange collar and green cuffs to 1808 then Kinski coatee, M. 1812 coatee from 1813. Shako with red wing and white cords, black plume tipped yellow, later red-orange plume and black tipped red-orange. Trumpeters: in 1808-09, red-orange Kinski coatee with sky blue collar, cuffs and turnbacks, white lace, sky blue overalls with red-orange stripe. About 1811, green coat with red-orange collar, cuffs, lapels and turnbacks, white buttonhole lace; Imperial livery from 1813.

25th: dolman with pink-red collar and cuffs to about 1804, coat to 1809 then Kinski coatee, M. 1812 coatee from 1813. Shako with pink-red wing and black and yellow plume, later green over pink-red. Officers had yellowish nankeen dolman and breeches for summer in early 1800s according to Marbot. Trumpeters: reversed colours.

26th: dolman with green collar and pink-red cuffs, coat also and later until 1809 then Kinski coatee, M. 1812 coatee from 1813. Green waistcoat with pink-red cuffs and white cords. Green over red plume, later green tipped red. Trumpeters: reversed colours.

27th (formed in May 1808 from Arrenberg's Belgian Light Horse): green dolman with pink-red collar and cuffs, yellow cords and brass buttons; green pelisse with black fur; green overalls, brown in Spain; yellow leather belts. From 1813, M. 1812 coatee with pink-red collar and green cuffs, pewter buttons. Trumpeters: reversed colours, green overalls, pink-red czapska.

28th (formed May 1808 from Tuscan Dragoons): green coatee with amaranth collar and cuffs, Kinski coatee from 1809, M. 1812 coatee from 1813. Shako with cockade at front instead of plate. Trumpeters: reversed colours with white lace, yellow plume; imperial livery from 1813.

29th (formed in Spain during 1810 from 3rd Provisional Light Cavalry): initially various uniforms and some brown Kinski coatees with red facings; eventually green M. 1812 coatee with green collar and amaranth cuffs. Green plume tipped amaranth. Trumpeters: reversed colours with white lace, yellow shako with green plume and white cords.

30th: this regiment, formed in Hamburg from 3 February 1811; converted to 9th Chevau-légers-lanciers on 18 June 1811; was initially to have amaranth collar and green cuffs but things worked out very differently. Available green cloth to make a Chasseur à cheval uniform was insufficient and since it was to be armed with lances, a lancer uniform was settled upon: green kurta with buff collar, pointed cuffs, lapels, turnbacks and piping; pewter buttons; red pantaloons with black stripe; czapska with red crown, white middle band, white metal sunrise plate, black leather chin strap; grey stable jacket with buff collar;

white accoutrements; red housings edged black; light cavalry sabre, pistols, carbine and lance with buff pennon. Officers: silver metal and lace; red mameluke-style pantaloon favoured. Trumpeters: red kurta, black collar, cuffs, lapels, turnbacks and piping edged with white lace, white epaulettes and trumpet cords; rest same as the men. The blue uniform of the 'Polish' chevau-légers-lanciers was only adopted in 1813 (see Chevau-légers-lanciers).

31st (formed in Portugal in September 1811 from 1st and 2nd Provisional Light Cavalry, was actually a lancer regiment): various uniforms at first then Polish kurta with buff collar and cuffs; pewter buttons; green sash with buff stripes, red for elite company; scarlet overalls with buff stripe for dress and green in the field; buff czapska, white band, white metal sunrise plate; buff over white lance pennant. Some may have had M. 1812 coatee in 1813-14. Trumpeters: same uniform as troopers with white lace at collar, cuffs and buttonholes, white epaulettes, plume yellow tipped green.

Chasseurs à Cheval de la Vendée

Mounted Chasseurs of Vendée. Created 5 June 1815; was to have up to four squadrons recruited with veterans in Vendée and lower Loire area for local service. Probably had only started its organization when news of Waterloo reached Vendée and disbanded.

Uniform: 'same as that of the Chasseurs à cheval, except that the collar and piping will be white and the shako will be replaced by...[blank].'

Chevau-Légers-Lanciers

The French cavalry had been surprised and impressed by the effectiveness of lancers as light cavalry in opposing armies. Noting this, the Emperor decreed, on 18 June 1811, the formation of nine regiments of 'Light Horse Lancers' by converting some regiments into lancers; each French regiment had four squadrons, the Polish six. The first six regiments were composed of French personnel of the 1st, 3rd, 8th, 9th, 10th and 29th Dragoons. The 7th and 8th were Poles of the Vistula Legion and the 9th was a mixture of Poles and Germans of the 30th Chasseurs à cheval and were disbanded 12 May 1814. The French regiments were disbanded after Waterloo in 1815.

Uniform of the French Light Horse Lancers: green coatee with collar, lapels, pointed cuffs and turnbacks of the facing colour, green eagle on the turnbacks, green shoulder straps piped with the facing colour, red epaulettes for elite company; brass buttons; green hussar breeches with yellow cords and green pantaloons with stripe of the facing colour, grey pantaloons also worn from 1813; hussar boots edged yellow; brass dragoon helmet with fur turban, brass comb and chin scales, black caterpillar crest on comb instead of mane as the dragoons, black visors in front and back, no plumes generally worn except elite companies which had red plumes (elite company of the 6th had red crest and white plume); gauntlet gloves; white cloak replaced in September 1811 by a green greatcoat; green stable jacket; facing colour forage cap with green upturn; sheepskin housings edged with facing colour. Armed with light cavalry sabre, pistols, carbine and a lance with red over white pennon. Officers: gold buttons, epaulettes and lace, gold belts with lines of the facing colour.

Trumpeters: no information on early dress except for 1st and 2nd shown with blue coatee with regimental facings, white lace edging facings, white epaulettes and caterpillar crest, white plume for 1st, red for 2nd; from 1812, green Imperial livery single-breasted coatee with facings edged by livery lace; white caterpillar crest on helmet but 6th shown with red crest in 1813-14.

Regimental facings: 1st, scarlet; 2nd, orange; 3rd, pink; 4th, crimson; 5th, sky blue; 6th, red.

Uniform of Polish Light Horse Lancers: blue kurta, collar, pointed cuffs, lapels, turnbacks and piping at back seams of regimental facing colour, blue shoulder straps piped with facing colour, white epaulettes for elite company; pewter buttons; blue sash with two white stripes; blue pantaloons with double stripes of facing colour; black boots; czapska with blue crown, piping and band of facing colour, brass plate, brass chain, white metal chin scales; red pointed pompon; crimson over white lance pennons; white sheepskin housings edged with the facing colour. Officers: silver buttons, epaulettes, lace and belts; czapska laced silver, gold plate and chain, white plume.

Trumpeters: initially kurta as the men, facings edged with silver lace; later green imperial livery with facings edged by livery lace.

Regimental facings: 7th, yellow; 8th, blue piped yellow cuffs and collar with yellow facings; 9th, buff.

Artillery, Specialists, Reserves and Navy

Corps Impérial de l'Artillerie

Imperial Corps of Artillery. When the French Revolution broke out, the Corps of Artillery consisted of seven army artillery regiments, six companies of miners, ten and later fifteen of 'Ouvriers' and a staff of specialist officers. In 1791, the colonial artillery was ordered amalgamated as the 8th regiment and, in April 1792, nine companies of light, or horse, artillery were raised and attached to the regiments. The horse artillery rapidly increased to 20 companies and, on 7 February 1794, organized into nine regiments, soon reduced to eight then to six in 1801. Eight artillery train battalions were attached since 1800 to each foot regiment. Two companies of 'Armuriers' (armourers

or gunsmiths) were added from 1805. It represented a force varying from 26,000 to 35,000 men. In 1813, a ninth foot artillery regiment was organized and the artillery train was now 14 battalions. This was reduced in 1814 to eight foot regiments, four of horse artillery, 12 companies of Ouvriers and four squadrons of artillery train.

Uniform of the Foot Artillery: blue coat, blue piped red lapels, cuff flaps and collar, red cuffs and red turnbacks with blue grenades, blue piped red shoulder straps; brass buttons; blue waistcoat and breeches; hat with red pompon replaced, from c. 1807, by the shako with brass plate and chin scales, red top band, cords and plume, also red pompon on campaign; blue greatcoat from 1806. From 1812, coatee in same colours as coat; blue waistcoat with red cuffs; shako without the red top band and with red pompon. White accoutrements, all gunners had the brass-hilted hanger with red sabre knot, dragoon musket with brass furnishings. Drummers: same as the men but red coat with blue collar, cuffs, lapels, wings and turnbacks edged with yellow lace; Imperial livery from 1812. Officers had gold metal and lace.

Uniform of the Ouvriers: same as the foot artillery but with red lapels; completely similar to the foot artillery from 1812.

Uniform of the Armuriers: same as the foot artillery but with blue piped red cuffs and red collar.

Uniform of the Horse Artillery: blue dolman with blue collar, red cuffs, red cords; brass buttons; blue and red sash; blue hussar-style waistcoat with red cords; blue hussar-style breeches with red cords; boots edged with red; blue overalls with red stripes; shako with brass plate and chin scales, red cords and plume; on campaign, blue coat with blue piped red pointed lapels, red pointed cuffs, red turnbacks with blue grenades, red epaulettes. From 1812, blue coatee with

Rear view of a gunner of the Horse Artillery of the line, c. 1800-1812. Print after Vernet.

Officer, Foot Artillery, c. 1805-1812. Miniature. J. Ostiguy, Ottawa.

blue piped red lapels, blue collar, red pointed cuffs, red turnbacks with blue grenades, red epaulettes; shako with red pompon, rest as before. Blue housings edged red with brass numeral, crossed cannons and grenade below. White accoutrements, brass hilted light cavalry sabre, carbine and pistols, blue sabretache edged red with brass crossed cannons, number and grenade. Trumpeters: same as the men but red dolman, blue cuffs and collar edged yellow, blue cords; also a variety of red coats with lapels sometimes worn with a czapska on campaign. Officers had the same as the men but with gold cords, buttons and lace.

Uniform of the Artillery Train: light grey-blue coatee, blue square lapels, collar, cuffs and turnbacks with light grey-blue grenades, light grey-blue piped blue shoulder straps; pewter buttons; light grey-blue also white waistcoat; light grey-blue overalls with blue stripe and white metal buttons; also buff breeches; boots; bicorn hat; grey cloak; hat and later shako with white metal plate and chin scales, white cords, grey-blue tipped red plume also pompon. From 1812, light grey-blue coatee, blue collar, cuffs, lapels and turnbacks, light grey-blue grenades on turnbacks; white metal buttons; light grey-blue waistcoat; buff

breeches; shako; green stable jacket; light grey-blue cloak. There were many variations such as sky blue instead of light grey-blue and white piping edging facings. Trumpeters: same but blue coatee with light grey-blue facings edged white; imperial livery from 1812. Officers had silver buttons, epaulettes, shako top band and cords.

Corps Impérial du Génie

Imperial Corps of Engineers. The French Corps of Engineers consisted of officers specialized in fortifications, of battalions of Sappers and companies of Miners with their own engineer officers, and of 'employees' serving as canal and building keepers. The corps had two sapper battalions raised to four in 1800 and six companies of miners; 5th sapper battalion and three miner companies raised 1801; each sapper battalion had nine companies of 152 each; miners organized into two miner battalions of five companies of 100 each on 21 December 1808; 6th sapper battalion raised in 1810 by incorporation of Dutch sappers; Walcheren sapper battalion created 4 May 1811; Ile d'Elbe (Elba) sapper battalion created 18 June 1811; company of 'Ouvriers' (Artisans) created 12 November 1811; reduced to five sapper battalions in 1813; reorganized into three regiments of two battalions each including five of sappers and one of miners on 12 May 1814; disbanded 15 October 1815 and later reorganized.

From 1 October 1806, each sapper battalion had 20 caissons for tools driven by 60 wagoneers ('charretiers') reorganized into four Train companies ('Train du Génie') totaling 563 on 11 August 1809; train battalion of six companies on 9 December 1811.

Uniform of Sapper Battalions: blue coat, black piped red collar, cuffs, cuff flaps and lapels, red turnbacks with blue crossed axes, blue piped red shoulder straps and red epaulettes; brass buttons; blue waistcoat and breeches; black and grey gaiters; bicorn hat with red plume or pompon, yellow cockade loop; white accoutrements; white stock in peacetime and black on campaign; grey greatcoat; short sabre with red sword knot; musket with brass furnishing. Shakos replaced hats from about 1808 but were officially ordered only on 9 November 1810. The shako had brass crowned eagle plate and chin scales, red plume and cords. Rank badges on sleeves were an orange lace for corporal, gold lace for sergeants. Miners had the same uniform as sappers except for orange epaulettes,

Opposite.

Gunner, Foot Artillery, c. 1808-1812. Print after Martinet. Anne S.K. Brown Military Collection, Brown University, Providence, USA.

Officer, Train of the Foot Artillery of the Line, c. 1812. Miniature.
J. Ostiguy, Ottawa.

Artillery Train on the march, c. 1805. Print after JOB.

shako cords and sabre knot. Drummers had the same uniform as the men but their facings were edged with orange lace before 1812, green Imperial livery thereafter. During sieges, the men in exposed positions could be issued an iron helmet and cuirass painted black.

The 1812 regulations kept the same uniform colours while introducing the coatee and a few changes: the turnbacks piped black; shoulder straps for sappers and orange epaulettes for miners; red pompon for shako.

Officers had the same uniform with gold metal, shako band, cords, pompon and sword knot, facings in black velvet, boots. Only the battalion officers wore the shako. The fortification and staff engineer officers wore the bicorn hat with gold cockade loop (no plume). Housings were blue laced gold. From 1807, engineer officers attached to cuirassier divisions were also to wear the cuirass.

Train uniform. The wagoneers from 1806 wore: light grey-blue coatee, black (no piping) pointed lapels and cuffs, white turnbacks; pewter buttons; white waistcoat; buff breeches; boots; bicorn hat; grey cloak; white accoutrements. Same uniform continued when they became Train in 1809 but a shako with white metal plate and chin scales would have been taken into wear. From 1812, light grey-blue coatee, black collar, cuffs, lapels and turnbacks, light grey-blue crowned 'N' on turnbacks; white metal buttons; light grey-blue waistcoat; buff breeches; shako; green stable jacket; light grey-blue cloak.

Ouvriers company uniform, from 1811: blue coatee, black piped red collar, cuffs and lapels, red turnbacks with blue grenades; brass buttons; blue waistcoat and breeches; shako with brass plate and chin scales, red pompon with small black aigrette; white accoutrements; blue greatcoat with black piped red collar. Work dress: blue round jacket, black collar and cuffs, brass buttons; blue or white linen trousers; blue fatigue cap piped red.

The 'employés' or keepers had the same uniform as the sappers but no plume on the bicorn, no epaulettes except for 1st class keepers who had them red with two gold cords; the 2nd class had two gold laces on the lower sleeves, 3rd class one gold lace, 4th class a gold lace on the upper sleeve.

Ingénieurs Géographes

Topographical engineers. Corps originated in 1777, abolished in 1791 but a staff of topographical engineers continued to exist. Reorganized as a corps of 90 officers from 30 January 1809.

Uniform: from 1809, blue coat, orange collar and cuffs (later blue piped orange), blue turnbacks piped orange; gold buttons and epaulettes; white waistcoat and breeches; plain bicorn hat.

Pontonniers

Pontoon troops, specialized in making temporary bridges to facilitate the crossing of rivers by armies. First battalion originated in Strasbourg in 1793; 2nd battalion raised in 1797; each battalion had eight companies; 1st battalion raised to ten companies while 2nd battalion reduced to six in 1808; Dutch pontonniers incorporated as 11th company of 2nd battalion on 31 October 1810 but disappeared in 1812 Russian campaign; 3rd battalion of six companies created on 18 April 1813; 1st raised to 14 companies in October 1813; 2nd raised to eight companies January 1814; 2nd and 3rd battalions disbanded on 12 May 1814; 1st disbanded in later 1815.

Uniforms. There appears to have been no specific orders on the early dress of these troops but iconography shows the following: blue coat, blue piped red collar, lapels, cuffs, cuff flaps and shoulder straps, red turnbacks; brass buttons; blue waistcoat and breeches; black gaiters with brass buttons; bicorn with red cockade loop and plume; white accoutrements. Later black shako with brass plate and chin scales, red top band, cords and plume. Gold metal and boots for officers. Variations include red cuffs instead of blue, red cuff flaps, piping on lapels only, red epaulettes. From 1811, the uniform was ordered to be the same as the foot artillery.

Canonniers Gardes-Côtes

Coast Guard Artillery. Raised 28 May 1803, 100 companies of gunners and 28 companies of auxiliary sedentary gunners; had risen to 140 companies by 1811 totalling about 17,000 men of which about half were mobilized permanently; disbanded on 20 April 1814 but 80 companies were raised again on 24 April 1815, disbanded on 14 August 1815.

Uniform decreed on 28 May 1803: blue coat with blue collar and cuffs, sea green lapels and piping; brass buttons; sea green waistcoat and breeches. On 1 September 1803, a new uniform was decreed: white coat with blue collar, cuffs, lapels and piping, red cuff flaps, white turnbacks; brass buttons; white waistcoat and breeches, plain bicorn, infantry musket with

Officer of the Topographical Engineers, 1810. Anne S.K. Brown Military Collection, Brown University, USA.

bayonet and cartridge box with sling. Vernet's and Viel de Castel's prints published a few years after the Empire depicted the blue faced sea green uniform with shakos. This might indicate that both uniforms were worn concurrently.

Pionniers Noirs

Battalion of Black Pioneers. Formed 11 May 1803 from three independent companies of French Black soldiers coming from the West Indies, often prisoners of war exchanged from England. The battalion was transferred to Neapolitan service on 14 August 1806 and became 'Royal-Africain'.

Uniform: brown coat, red cuffs and lapels, white turnbacks; brass buttons; white waistcoat and breeches.

Pionniers Coloniaux

Colonial Pioneers. Four battalions created 3 August 1811, attached to the Colonial Battalions posted in Europe; disciplinary unit; amalgamated into a two-battalion colonial depot on 5 October 1814.

Uniform: 'The dress of these troops will consist in

French Pontoon troops and 'Mariniers' (sailors), c. 1810. The first and third figures are of Pontoon troops and wear all blue coats with red piping, brass buttons and shako plates. The second and fourth figure are sailors from a naval battalion attached to the army to man the boats. They wear shakos, blue single breasted jackets piped red with brass buttons, blue and white pantaloons. Print after Berka and Zimner. Anne S.K. Brown Military Collection, Brown University, USA.

a pantaloon, a [sleeveless] waistcoat, a single-breasted round jacket, half gaiters, a forage cap and a greatcoat...all to be light grey-blue...The officers,

NCOs and corporals to wear the long-tailed coat in the same colour...'

Medical Services

The medical services in the armies of this period were not numerous and not considered of great importance. Typically, the French army, in spite of its great size, had few medical officers. About a thousand surgeons in 1804, a number that doubled in a few years but the newcomers had deplorable medical training. Doctors were few and surgeons formed the majority. On 13 April 1809, ten companies of 'infirmiers' recruited

Coast Guard Artillery, gunner, 1810. This print shows the blue uniform with sea green facings shown at the collar. The breeches are shown blue. The epaulettes and shako pompon are red. Note the anchor and crossed cannons badge on the cartridge box. Print after Vernet.

from mutilated volunteers were organized. Their duty was to get the wounded out to the field hospitals and give first aid.

Dress uniform from 1803 for Medical Officers serving in military hospitals: medium blue single-breasted coat with nine buttons in front, medium blue lining, no epaulettes, black velvet collar and cuffs for medical doctors, scarlet for surgeons, green for pharmacists; gold buttons; waistcoat was the colour of the coat's facings; medium blue breeches; boots; bicorn with gold cockade loop; medium blue cloak with cape edged with gold lace; medium blue housings edged with a gold lace, width depending on rank. For undress, the uniform was similar but with a stand and fall collar and cuffs slashed under but these features, ordered during the Consulate, do not seem to have been implemented widely at the time of the Empire.

The various grades of medical officers were distinguished as follows:

Inspector General: double gold lace edging collar,

Coast Guard Artillery, gunner, 1810. Print after JOB from a drawing by B. de Valmont.

cuffs, pockets and front of coat and waistcoat. Lace on collar and cuffs only for undress.

Chief Doctor, Surgeon or Pharmacist: single gold lace edging collar, cuffs, pockets and front of coat and waistcoat. Lace on collar and cuffs only for undress.

Professor: nine wide gold buttonhole lace in front of coat, two at each side of collar and three to each cuff and pocket on dress coat. Waistcoat edged with

Pharmacist 2d class J.-F. Fontaine, Medical Corps, c. 1803-1812. Print after miniature.

'Infirmier' of the Medical Corps, 1812. Print after Vernet.

gold lace. Buttonholes on collar and cuffs only for undress, lace edging waistcoat.

Doctor: nine gold buttonhole lace in front of coat, two at each side of collar and three to each cuff and pocket on dress coat. Waistcoat edged with gold lace. Buttonholes on collar and cuffs only for undress.

First Class: nine gold buttonhole lace in front of coat, two at each side of collar and three to each cuff and pocket on dress coat. Buttonholes on collar and cuffs only for undress.

Second Class: two at collar and three to each cuff and pocket on dress coat. Buttonholes on collar only for undress.

Third Class: two at collar and three to each cuff on dress coat. One buttonholes on collar only for undress.

Students had the same uniforms but without any lace or embroidery.

From 1812, lapels of the facing colour were added.

Regimental surgeons were to wear the same uniform with the regimental buttons but they often wore the regimental uniform with crimson (rather than scarlet) velvet cuffs and collars with the gold embroidery of their grade but with no epaulettes.

Medical officers in the Imperial Guard had gold aiguillettes.

Uniform of the 1809 'Infirmiers': brown coatee, red piped white collar, pointed cuffs, pointed lapels and turnbacks; brass buttons; white breeches; bicorn hat with brown plume tipped red, later shako with brass plate and chin scales, red pompon.

Artistes Vétérinaires
Veterinary 'Artists'. From 7 February 1812, they were assigned a uniform: all blue single breasted coat, two small buttons under each cuff, two silver buttonholes at each side of the collar and at the cuffs; buttons and turnback ornaments in gold or silver depending on the veterinarian's regiment, no epaulettes; buff breeches and high boots in heavy cavalry and train, pantaloons of regimental coat colour and hussar boots in light cavalry and light artillery; regimental cloak; bicorn; regimental sabre.

National Guards, Gendarmerie and Constabulary
Napoleon's extensive talents to organize and militarize all sorts of forces is exemplified by the creation of a large reserve army, the militarization of police units

National Guard levies of 1814 in battle wearing the blue smock.
Print after Raffet.

and the creation or transformation of civil service units into constabulary and para-military corps.

Garde Nationale

National Guards. In 1789, National Guard units sprang up all over France replacing the militia and, to some extent, constabulary forces. Many were converted into active units or faded away during the 1790s so that when Napoleon came to power, the institution was all but nonexistent as an effective force. In 1805, the National Guard was completely restructured and organized in battalion-like cohorts (ten companies each including grenadiers and chasseurs). They were to assist in the maintenance of interior order, provide garrisons in forts and patrol the frontiers. In 1806, 31 legions each having four cohorts were mobilized; 1807, five 'Légions de réserve de l'intérieur' were formed for active duty, each having six cohorts and an artillery company; cohorts reorganized into eight

National Guard infantry private, 1807. The uniform was similar to the line infantry except for white metal buttons. Print after Martinet.

companies each, six of fusiliers, one of artillery and one of depot in March 1812, companies of voltigeurs and grenadiers organized later; many National Guards were mobilized on 12 January 1813 and used to form the 137th, and the 145th to 150th regiments of line infantry, the artillery companies into line artillery. More National Guard cohorts were raised during 1813 in various areas and a mass levy of National Guards ordered in many departments in March 1814, the units resulting being known under a variety of names; all released from service after Napoleon's abdication; National Guard ordered again from early April 1815 and disbanded after Waterloo.

Uniform: infantry same as line infantry but pewter buttons, silver for officers. Artillery same as line artillery but blue collar and pewter buttons.

Supplies of uniforms low from 1813; by February 1814, militiamen mobilized were to assemble in Paris where they would be armed and issued 'a shako, a cartridge box, a greatcoat, a knapsack, and if possible, a pair of breeches, a coatee or a sleeved jacket.' By March, the contingents were to be issued with blue blouses, shakos, shoes and black accoutrements; officers and NCOs distinguished by embroidery on the collar. This could vary as National Guards organized by Marshal Davout in Hamburg during February 1814 had no uniform but all wore bicorn hats and had a white armband with 'Garde nationale' in black letters, officers had white sashes. Meanwhile, some mounted volunteer units in the Ardennes and Alsace went so far as to dress like Russian Cossacks!

The 1815 National Guards were to have the blue blouse as the standard dress, grenadiers and voltigeurs in full uniform if possible, officers in uniform if they wished or the blouse. Mobilized companies were to have military muskets, sedentary companies with hunting muskets, black accoutrements. Uniformity could vary greatly from one place to the other. For instance, the National Guards of the Cher turned out in full uniforms in 1815 while their neighbors in the Loiret mustered with shakos, blue blouses with red cuffs and collars, and blue pantaloons.

Corps Francs

Free Corps. Created 22 April 1815; corps to be organized in border departments, numbered by seniority; infantry corps to each have a maximum of 1000 men, cavalry units to be 300 lancers each; dissolved after Waterloo.

Uniform: 'these corps will not be obliged to have any regular uniform' and armed 'indifferently of military or hunting muskets' and the cavalry to have lances without pennon.

Tirailleurs Fédérés

Federated Sharpshooters. Created 15 May 1815; 24 battalions raised in Paris and viscinity from men not enrolled in the National Guard; each battalion had 720 men divided into six companies; companies assembled every Sunday; were to garrison fortifications around Paris if called to active duty; dissolved after Waterloo.

Uniform: civilian clothing, black accoutrements and muskets.

Colonial National Guards

The French overseas colonies all had auxiliary forces organized as local National Guards. In Martinique, a decree of 14 October 1802 specified that all whites and free Blacks from ages 16 to 55 were to be enrolled; six battalions each with Grenadier and Chasseurs companies and the rest of Fusiliers.

Uniform of white companies: blue coat, lapels and lining, red collar and cuffs, white piping; brass buttons; white waistcoat and gaiter-trousers; round hat, white cockade loop, red, white and blue plume for Fusiliers, red plume, cockade loop, red epaulettes and grenades on the turnbacks for Grenadiers; green plumes, cockade loop, epaulettes and bugle horns on the turnbacks for Chasseurs. Black companies had the same but wore coatees. Dragoon companies attached to each battalion and had blue frock with white collar, red cuffs and piping, yellow epaulettes; brass ball buttons; white waistcoat, blue pantaloons, knee boots, round hat with yellow cockade loop and a white plume with a black base; housings blue edged with red lace. Officers had gold metal and epaulettes.

Guadeloupe had six battalions of National Guards from 1802, each battalion having white Fusilier companies, coloured Chasseur companies and a company of dragoons. Infantry apparently had the French 'National uniform' (same as line infantry) but with white collar and cuffs instead of red.

The National Guard of Ile-de-France (Mauritius) and La Réunion reorganized from October to December 1803; whites 'infanterie' companies of 64 men each. Free Blacks formed 24 men sections of 'Chasseurs coloniaux' attached to the white companies; Artillery detachments for some companies in Ile-de-France, three companies at La Réunion. 'Chasseurs de réserve' created 2 June 1806 composed of trusty slaves with white planters as officers, later known also as 'Bataillon africain' (African Battalions) when mobilized. 'Compagnie de Mahé' National Guard created 15 May 1807, had two white infantry sections and a Black chasseur section.

Mounted and dismounted members of the Imperial
Gendarmerie in various orders of dress, c. 1804-1815. Print after
Marbot.

Uniforms: white 'infanterie' companies of Ile-de-France and La Réunion had the 'National uniform'; 'Chasseurs coloniaux', blue coatee, lapel and turnbacks, red collar and cuffs, white piping, pewter buttons. The gunners, blue coatee, lapels and turnbacks, red collar, cuffs and piping; brass buttons. 'Chasseurs de réserve' officers, green coatee, cuffs and turnbacks, black collar, silver buttons and epaulettes; white waistcoat and pantaloons; sergeant-majors had blue coatee, cuffs and turnbacks, green collar, pewter buttons; white waistcoat and breeches; black gaiters; the slaves had no uniform. Seychelles National Guard Company in Mahé white sections, blue coat, lapels and turnbacks piped red with red collar and cuffs piped white, brass buttons; Black section, blue coatee and lapels piped green, green collar, cuffs and turn-backs, pewter buttons. All wore shakos made locally of cloth on a wicker frame and considered far better than hats. Finally, the British observed some militias at La Réunion and Mauritius in 1809-10 wearing white uniforms with blue facings.

Gendarmerie

Gendarmerie Impériale

The national police force of the Ancien Régime, the 'Maréchaussée', was reorganized as the 'Gendarmerie Nationale' in 1791 and became a completely military organization. The Gendarmerie ('impériale' from 1804) could serve as local police or be deployed with the army, not only to watch for lawless soldiers but as a combat force.

Uniform of mounted gendarmes: blue coat, red collar, cuffs, lapels and turnbacks with blue grenade, white aiguillettes ending trefoil on left shoulder, blue edged red shoulder strap at right; pewter buttons; yellow-buff waistcoat and breeches; high black boots; bicorn edged white, red plume; yellow-buff belts edged white; blue cloak; blue housings edged white with white grenade, white sheepskin with red edging. Armed with straight-bladed sabre, pistols and carbine. Foot gendarmes: same uniform but with long black gaiters; armed like grenadiers with infantry hanger, musket and bayonet. Officers: silver metal and lace. Trumpeters and drummers: same coat as the men with a silver lace edging collar, cuffs and turnbacks.

Gendarmerie d'Espagne

Gendarmerie of Spain. Corps of 4000 French personnel including 2000 gendarmes detached for service in Spain; 20 squadrons each of 200 men (including 80 mounted) raised from January 1810; a legion of 1400 men raised to serve in Catalonia from June 1810; legion for Burgos formed in November 1810; force reorganized into six legions in December 1812; saw much action; dissolved on evacuation of Spain in late 1813.

Uniform: same as above but red epaulettes with strap edged white for foot gendarmes. Brown Spanish cloth was often used for uniform repairs and replacements on the spot.

Lanciers Gendarmes

Lancer Gendarmes. Formed in Spain at the end of 1810 by training two squadrons of mounted gendarmes in Aragon to use lances and light cavalry tactics, then attached to various other squadrons. Disbanded in 1814.

Uniform: blue coat, blue piped red pointed lapels, red collar, pointed cuffs and turnbacks, white aiguillette; pewter buttons; red hussar waistcoat, white cords; blue hussar breeches with white cords; boots edged white; black shako, white metal plate and chin scales, red plume; white belts; red over white

Inspector General Buquet of the Gendarmerie. His uniform, as a senior officer, was the blue faced scarlet of the Gendarmerie embroidered with silver. Print after portrait.

lance pennon; blue housings edged with white lace and white grenade. Buglers: same but coat is all red with white epaulettes; blue hussar waistcoat; white shako plume.

Gendarmerie Impériale de Paris

Created 10 April 1813 to replace the 'Garde de Paris' (see below) which had been amalgamated into the line infantry and the Imperial Guard; four companies totaling 853 men, part mounted, part foot; reorganized as 'Garde royale de Paris' on 31 May and 14 August 1814.

Uniform: same as the Gendarmerie Impériale but buttons, belt-plates and other insignia marked to the corps with coat of arms of the city; red edged silver bandoleer with silver plate bearing coat of arms; red edged silver sword-belt worn over the shoulder; 2nd class gendarmes had white accoutrements instead and unlaced hat; 'élèves-gendarmes' (student-gendarmes) had a grenadier's shako with red band, cords and plume, red epaulettes, grenadier's arms and accoutrements.

Gendarmerie Coloniale

Colonial Gendarmerie. Some French overseas colonies had small units of Gendarmes, serving on foot, until 1810 when the last colonies fell to the British. Martinique had a company from 1802, dressed as in France but with white piping edging the facings, yellow nankeen waistcoat and gaiter-trousers, no lace on the bicorn hat. In Saint-Domingue (Haiti), a company was organized from December 1802 with the same uniform as in France except that the coat was a short-tailed coatee and a round hat with white cockade loop and red plume. French Guyana had, from 1803, a Company of Black Gendarmes dressed as best as could be with limited resources. Ile-de-France (Mauritius) and La Réunion also had a small Gendarmerie from March 1808 dressed as in France but with yellow nankeen waistcoat and breeches, gaiters or half-boots.

Garrison and Constabulary Troops

Garde de Paris

Paris Guard. The security of the City of Paris traditionally depended on a military constabulary force. During the French Revolution, this became disorganized and Gendarmerie detachments filled in. On 4 October 1802, Napoleon created two infantry regiments, two battalions each, and a squadron of dragoons of two companies as 'a municipal guard of the city of Paris' shortened to 'Garde de Paris' in 1806; provided service battalions which campaigned with the Grande Armée; both regiments amalgamated into a single two-battalion regiment on 12 February 1812; infantry converted into 134th Line Regiment in October 1812; dragoons amalgamated to 2nd Lancers of the Imperial Guard.

Uniform from 1802: 1st Regiment, green coat, red collar, cuffs and lapels, red cuff flaps piped green, white turnbacks; brass buttons; white waistcoat and breeches; black gaiters. 2nd Regiment: red coat, green collar, cuffs and lapels, green cuff flaps piped red, white turnbacks; brass buttons; white waistcoat and breeches; black gaiters; infantry accoutrements and arms. Grenadiers of 1st regiment: bearskin cap with brass plate, green plume and white or green cords, red or green epaulettes with red crescent; 2nd had similar bearskin cap with white cords, red plume and epaulettes; on campaign, shako with red plume and cords. Voltigeurs had a bearskin cap without plate, green plume sometimes tipped yellow, green or white cords, shako on campaign, yellow-buff collar and epaulettes. Fusiliers had bicorns with company pompon, coat colour shoulder straps piped red or green. Drummer had the men's uniform with facings

Grenadier, 1st Regiment of the Garde de Paris, c. 1807. Sketch after Weiland.

Officer, 2nd Regiment of the Garde de Paris, c. 1807. Sketch after Weiland.

edged with gold lace.

From 1808: 1st Regiment, white coat, green collar, cuffs, lapels and turnbacks with white ship (the badge of Paris), white piped green cuff flaps, white piping edging facings; brass buttons. 2nd Regiment, same with red facings. Grenadiers, bearskin as before, red cords and plume, white grenade on turnbacks, red epaulettes. Voltigeurs, bearskin as before, white cords, green plume tipped yellow, yellow-buff collar, green

epaulettes with yellow crescent for 1st and red for 2nd, white bugle horn on turnback. Fusiliers, shako with white cords and company pompon, white shoulder straps piped green or red. From 1812, the amalgamated regiment adopted the white and green uniform of the former 1st.

Dragoons, 1802-1812: light grey-blue coat, red collar, cuffs and lapels, light grey-blue turnbacks; pewter buttons; yellow-buff waistcoat and breeches;

Grenadier, 34th Departmental Legion, 1813. Print after contemporary illustration.

hussar boots; brass dragoon helmet with black mane and red plume for 1st company, red over black for 2nd; white accoutrements; dragoon musket and sword; light grey-blue sleeved cloak; light grey-blue housings laced white. Trumpeters: red coat with sky blue collar, cuffs, lapels and turnbacks, white lace at lapel buttonholes and edging collar; pewter buttons; helmet with white mane, red plume and leopard fur turban; red trumpet cords; sky blue housings laced white.

Compagnies de Réserve des Départements

Departmental Reserve Companies. Also called 'Légions départementales de réserve'. Created 14 May 1805. Prefects in each department raised these companies meant to stand guard at prefectures, departmental archives, poor hospices and jails. Companies were to have from 36 up to 250 men each. They were organized into 28 'legions' with, usually, the companies of four departments grouped into a legion. From 1808, some reserve companies were detached to armies for active service; disbanded 31 May 1814.

Uniform, decreed on 18 August 1805: sky blue coat, vertical pockets, white turnbacks; brass buttons; white waistcoat and breeches; a pair of grey and a pair of black gaiters; black cravat; bicorn hats; grey or beige greatcoat; infantry arms and equipment. Each group of seven legions had facing colours applied differently. The parts of the facings not designated were of the coat colour piped with the facing colour.

Collar, cuffs and lapels:

1st, white; 2nd, red; 3rd, green; 4th, yellow; 5th, orange; 6th, crimson; 7th, black.

Collar and lapels:

8th, white; 9th, red; 10th, green; 11th, yellow; 12th, orange; 13th, crimson; 14th, black.

Cuffs and lapels:

15th, white; 16th, red; 17th, green; 18th, yellow; 19th, orange; 20th, crimson; 21st, black.

Lapels:

22nd, white; 23rd, red; 24th, green; 25th, yellow; 26th, orange; 27th, crimson; 28th, black.

Notice of the change in headgear to shakos was sent to the departments in November 1807 but specified that bicorns were to be worn out first.

On 20 July 1808, the colour of the coat was changed to white. The companies that had white facings now had sky blue facings, the other companies keeping the same colours.

As the size of the French Empire increased and the new territories organized into departments, new legions came into being. The 29th Legion (Italy) created 6 September 1810 had pink collar, cuffs and lapels; the 30th (Italy) created 9 May 1811 had sky blue collar and cuffs; the 31st (Illyrian provinces) was not formed; 32nd, green collar and cuffs; 33rd, yellow collar and cuffs; 34th, orange collar and cuffs. The last three legions were in western Germany. Their waistcoat had collars and cuffs of the facing colour.

The changes in cut and style in the 1812 dress regulation were also directed towards the Departmental Legions. The draft regulation also contained some changes in the legion's uniform facing colours. Some of these changes were implemented but it is hard to say how widely in a period of turmoil and collapse of the empire during 1813-1814. In each series, the 1st Legion had sky blue facings, the 2nd red, 3rd green, 4th yellow, 5th orange, 6th crimson and 7th black.

The first series of Legions 1 to 7 had collar, lapels, cuffs, turnbacks and shoulder straps of the facing colour, white cuff flaps piped with the facing colour.

The second series, Legions 8 to 14, had collar, lapels, shoulder straps and turnbacks of the facing colour, sky blue cuffs, white cuff flaps piped in the facing colour.

The third series, Legions 15 to 21, had cuffs, lapels, shoulder straps and turnbacks of the facing colour, sky blue collar (except for 15th Legion which had white piped sky blue collar), white cuff flaps piped in the facing colour.

The fourth series, Legions 22 to 28, had cuffs, lapels and turnbacks of the facing colour, sky blue collar and shoulder straps (except for 22nd Legion which had white piped sky blue collar and shoulder straps), white cuff flaps piped in the facing colour.

The 29th had pink collar, cuffs, lapels, turnbacks and shoulder straps, white piped pink cuff flaps. The 30th had the same facings in sky blue, the 32nd had green facings, the 33rd had yellow, the 34th had orange.

Douaniers

Customs. Personnel of the customs, often recruited from veteran soldiers, also acted as border guards. Soon after Napoleon came to power, the 'Douaniers' were given a military organization, a uniform and armed; mounted brigades added in 1812; some customs personnel organized into temporary infantry battalions in 1814.

Uniform: from 1801, all green single-breasted coat; pewter buttons; green or white waistcoat, green pantaloons; black light infantry gaiters edged white; bicorn with silver cockade loop, sometimes with green pompon and red brush. Rank was denoted by a complex system, senior officials had silver embroidery on collar and cuffs and, for very senior staff, pocket flaps, silver lace for officers and white lace for the men. White piping sometimes used. Some had the shako with white metal plate, white or silver cord, green plume tipped red from c. 1810. Short sabre, musket and bayonet, white accoutrements. Mounted brigades from 1812 had the coat front, turnbacks and pointed cuffs piped white, collar had a green three-pointed patch with a button at the centre, white trefoils on shoulders; green hussar waistcoat with white cords; green hussar breeches with white cords; hussar boots edged white; bicorn with silver tassels, white plume with green lower third; white chasseur à cheval accoutrements; carbine and light cavalry sabre.

Sapeurs-Pompiers de Paris

Firemen-sappers of Paris. This organization was increasingly militarized once Napoleon came to power. It had three companies of 100 men each from 1801; raised to a five company battalion of 576 men on 18 September 1811 and armed with short sabre, musket with bayonet; white accoutrements.

Uniform: blue coat, black piped red collar, cuffs

Customs agent, Douanes Impériales, c. 1804-1815. Print after Vernet.

and lapels, blue turnbacks, blue shoulder straps piped red; brass buttons; blue round jacket with black collar; blue breeches; black gaiters, later light infantry gaiters edged red; brass helmet with leather turban, brass eagle in front, brass comb, black caterpillar crest, black plume tipped red.

Veterans and Invalids

Before the French Revolution, soldiers too old or unfit for active duty but equal to garrison service were assigned to companies of invalids posted in forts and fortresses. On 16 May 1792, the invalids were renamed 'Vétérans nationaux'; 'Vétérans impériaux' from 17 May 1805 of 90 companies of 120 men each and 25 gunner companies of 100 men each from September 1805; other veteran's companies were added as the Empire amalgamated other areas.

Uniform: blue faced red until organization into Half-Brigades in 1800 when the line infantry uniform was adopted. From May 1805, the infantry veterans had blue coat with blue cuffs, red collar, cuff flaps and lapels, white turnbacks with blue stars, blue piped red shoulder straps; pewter buttons; white waistcoat and

1st class artisan of the Navy's 'Ouvriers militaires de la Marine' between 1810-1814. Print after Vernet.

the Navy had its own artillery regiments and 'Ouvriers' battalions as well as Gendarmerie, naval engineers and a host of administrative and security forces, all with distinctive uniforms, which are far too numerous to deal with here. With sailors added, the Navy could number up to 100,000 men, a considerable force which Napoleon partly mobilized to serve on land.

Artillerie de la Marine

Marine Artillery. The Royal Marine Artillery Corps was disbanded in the turmoil of the Revolution but the government soon came to its senses. On 25 October 1795, a new corps of Marine Artillery of 22,000 men in 7 Half-Brigades was created, each having three battalions of nine companies, each company having 120 men; also three companies of 'Ouvriers' of the marine artillery and four squads of 'Apprentis-canonniers' (apprentice gunners) to provide trained gunners for the fleet. Corps transformed into four regiments totaling 14,400 men on 5 May 1803; four companies of 'Ouvriers', each of 150 men; 5th and 6th companies added in May and June 1805; four companies of 'Apprentis-canonniers', three more from 6 October 1803; one disbanded in 1805; titled 'Corps impérial de l'Artillerie de la Marine' on 9 November 1804; establishment raised on 29 February 1812 to 19,500 strong; transferred from the Ministry of the Navy to the Ministry of War on 24 January 1813. Six battalions remained in the ports, 20 battalions totaling 9640 men became the outstanding 'Marine Division' of the 1813-14 campaigns; rallied to the Emperor in 1815 but saw no action.

Uniform from 1803: blue coat, blue piped scarlet cuffs, lapels and turnbacks; red collar piped white and red cuff flap; brass buttons; blue waistcoat and breeches; black gaiters. First Class gunners had red epaulettes, Second Class gunners had red shoulder straps, 'Aspirants' gunners blue piped red shoulder straps. NCOs and master gunners had a gold lace edging the collar. Bicorn hat with a yellow cockade loop and red pompon; from 1807, black shako with red cords and pompon (red plume for dress occasions), brass plate, red bands at the top and base until c. 1810, black thereafter. Blue undress 'paletot' and linen pantaloons; white accoutrements; hanger only worn by NCOs and First Class gunners; musket with brass furnishings. 'Ouvriers' had the same uniform except for scarlet lapels. 'Apprentis-canonniers' had a blue 'paletot' and a leather cap with brass plate bearing 'the attributes of the artillery'. During the 1813 and 1814 campaigns, the four artillery regiments were sometimes mistaken for the Imperial Guard as they

breeches; bicorn with white cockade loop and red pompon; infantry arms and equipment with short sabre; infantry shako with white metal diamond-shaped plate and chin scales from November 1810; crowned N on turnbacks and lapels to waist from 1812. Artillery companies wore the same uniform as the line artillery.

There were also invalids at the hospital of the 'Invalides' in Paris. Napoleon added hospitals at Louvain and Avignon as well as care homes at Versailles and Vincennes. These men were truly invalidated by missing limbs, blindness or affected by other grievous wounds and cared for by Medical Corps staff and nursing nuns. Their uniform was an ample blue coat with no lapels, open in front, small blue standing collar, red round cuffs and lining; pewter buttons; blue waistcoat and breeches; bicorn with white cockade loop. There also were many badges for various ranks and decorations.

Navy

The French Navy was not part of the army but was under the authority of the Ministry of the Navy. But

Admiral's dress uniform, c. 1804-1815. Senior naval officers of the French Imperial Navy had similar uniforms to army generals, blue with gold embroidery. The only distinction was the anchor badge on buttons, belt-plates and belt.

wore blue greatcoats with blue pantaloons and black shako covers. Officers had gold metal and lace.

Ouvriers Militaires de la Marine

Military Artisans of the Navy. Raised on 15 January 1808, of 18 companies augmented to several battalions; 11 battalions existing in 1811; most served with the land army; disbanded during May of 1814, re-raised in May 1815 and disbanded in July and August.

Uniform: blue coatee with black velvet collar, cuffs and lapels, blue piped red turnbacks piped red with an anchor and crossed axes as ornaments; brass buttons; blue waistcoat and breeches; long grey gaiters; shako with red bands and pompon, also red over black plume, and yellow cockade loops. 1st class Ouvriers had red fringed epaulettes, 2nd class red shoulder straps and 3rd class blue shoulder straps piped red. Working dress was a fatigue cap, 'paletot' and trousers all in dark blue with black short gaiters as well as a linen smock and trousers. Officers: gold buttons, epaulettes and lace.

Back view of Admiral's dress uniform, c. 1804-1815.

Gendarmerie Maritime

Maritime or naval Gendarmerie. Seven companies posted in large naval bases and arsenal at Brest, Lorient, Le Havre, Rochefort, Toulon, Antwerp and Genoa.

Uniform: same as the Gendarmerie but buttons had naval designations and anchor. Some also mention an anchor on belt-plate and at the collar.

Équipages de la Flotille Nationale

The 'Équipages' were simply the crew of each ship. Although they had no set uniform initially, they generally were issued a 'paletot' which was a double breasted round jacket with standing collar, a waistcoat, long trousers, a wool cap and a round hat. In May 1804, sailors were henceforth to wear a blue jacket with horn buttons, red waistcoat, blue trousers, black cravat and round hat.

The 'Flotille Nationale' came about from late May 1803 when Napoleon started planning an invasion of England. Within a few months, the 'Flotille Nationale' had over 20,000 men which remained poised to attempt a crossing for the next two years. The 'Flotille' sailor's uniform was ordered to be, from

July 1803, a blue 'paletot' with scarlet collar, cuff flaps and arm band; brass buttons; blue or white trousers; round hat.

Équipages de Haut-Bord, Équipages de Flotille

Crews of ships of the line, crews of flotillas. After Trafalgar, Napoleon had little time to devote to the Navy with campaigns in Austria and Germany. In 1808 however, the Emperor's renewed attention to the fleet brought sweeping changes. On 8 March, all ship's crews were reorganized into 50 numbered 'Bataillons de la Marine impériale' soon renamed 'Équipages de Haut-Bord' followed by gunboat crews on 7 April who were formed into battalion-like 'Équipages de Flotille' each crew having 500 men divided into four companies. Greeted with much grumbling in the ports, the new organization nevertheless grew considerably. By 1811, there were 63 'Haut-Bord' and 22 Flotilla crews; in 1812, 76 'Haut-Bord' and 24 Flotilla; in March 1813, both types of crews were combined for a total of 110; in January 1814, ship's crews were ordered to send 120 men skilled in artillery to serve with the army; all crews disbanded after Napoleon's 1814 abdication. On his return from Elba, he ordered 40 'équipages de Haut-Bord' raised in April 1814, each having four companies of fusiliers with one of grenadiers and one of voltigeurs; saw no action and disbanded after Waterloo.

Uniform of the 'Haut-Bord' from April 1808: blue 'paletot' with collar, cuffs, shoulder straps and piping of distinctive facing colours for each 'équipage' or crew; brass buttons; blue waistcoat; blue or white trousers; grey linen gaiters; black cravat; shako with brass plate, white cords, pompon of the facing colour. The shako caused considerable scorn from the sailors and were replaced, from August 1811, by a round hat having a brass scroll with the crew's designation in front, cockade on the side and pompon of the facing colour. The NCOs had the regular military blue coat with blue pointed lapels with facings and piping of the distinctive colour. It should be noted that period illustrations show many variations to the above general rules. The facings of the first 53 crews are known and were as follows:

Crew	Collar, cuffs, shoulder straps	Piping
1	Blue	Red
2	Blue	Green
3	Blue	Orange
4	Sky blue	Sky blue
5	Blue	Light green
6	Blue	Yellow
7	Sky blue	Blue
8	Blue	Pink
9	Red	Red
10	Red	Blue
11	Red	Sky blue
12	Red	Green
13	Red	Orange
14	Dark yellow	Sky blue
15	Blue	White
16	Red	Light green
17	Dark yellow	White
18	Dark yellow	White
19	Red	Yellow
20	Red	White
21	Red	Pink
22	Red	Violet
23	Dark yellow	Light green
24	Dark yellow	Pink
25	Dark yellow	Violet
26	Dark yellow	Green
27	Orange	Orange
28	Orange	White
29	Orange	Blue
30	Green	White
31	Dark yellow	Blue
32	Dark yellow	Red
33	Sky blue	Red
34	Sky blue	Green
35	Sky blue	Orange
36	Sky blue	Violet
37	Sky blue	Light Green
38	Sky blue	Yellow
39	Sky blue	White
40	Sky blue	Pink
41	Orange	Sky blue
42	Orange	Pink
43	Orange	Light green
44	Orange	Green
45	Green	Green
46	Green	Red
47	Green	Orange
48	Green	Violet
49	Green	Yellow
50	Green	Pink
51	Green	Blue
52	Green	Sky blue
53	Violet	Blue

The 1815 crews had the same uniform as before but without facing colours.

Uniform of the 'équipages de Flotille' or Flotilla crews, 1808-1813: same as the 'Haut-Bord' but all with blue facings and piping.

Accoutrements for all crews were to be the same as

French sailors in Hamburg, 1813. They wear round hats with red pompons, all blue 'paletots' with red epaulettes which may indicate they belong to the elite company of an 'équipage de Flotille' (Flotilla Crew), blue trousers, red waistcoat visible at the neck, brass buttons, black accoutrements. The officer wears a blue surtout with gold epaulettes and buttons. Print after Christoph Suhr. Anne S.K. Brown Military Collection, Brown University, USA.

for army troops but there were variations as the 9th had black belting in 1814. Muskets were of naval models, almost similar to army muskets but with brass furnishings.

Officers wore the uniforms prescribed for naval officers and did not use the distinctive crew facings. They conformed to an extensive regulation of 1804. Briefly, the dress uniform was blue, single breasted with nine buttons, scarlet collar and cuffs, blue lining, gold buttonhole embroidery bearing an anchor design at collar, cuffs, front and pocket flaps for ship of the line captain and variable arrangements for lower commissioned rank, gold epaulettes; gold buttons; white waistcoat; blue or white breeches; bicorn hat with gold cockade loop.

Foreign Troops

The French Army always had an important contingent of foreign mercenary troops. The annexation of vast territories into the Empire brought many more into the Imperial Army, achieving a transnational character not seen since the Roman Army. It also brought some most unusual uniforms into the French Napoleonic Army. We only include the main units existing during the Imperial era.

Switzerland

Demi-Brigades Suisses

Swiss Half Brigades. In December 1798, an agreement between France and the Swiss Cantons called for a levy of 18,000 Swiss to form six Helvetic Half Brigades, reduced to three in January 1800. The 3rd was sent to Haiti in 1803 and eventually incorporated into the 5th Light Infantry. The 1st sent a detachment to Guadeloupe which remained distinct until 1808. The Half Brigades were incorporated into the new 1st Swiss Regiment in 1805 (see below).

Uniform: the Half Brigades raised from 1798 had a blue coat with yellow piped red cuffs and lapels, red piped yellow collar, green piped yellow cuff flaps, white turnbacks, yellow piping edging pocket flaps; pewter buttons; white waistcoat and breeches; bicorn hat with green, red and yellow cockade and plume. By a decree of 31 March 1803, the Half Brigades were assigned red coats with red collar, white lining; pewter buttons; white waistcoat and breeches; hat with French cockade and no plume. The 1st had white cuffs and lapels with blue piping, the 2nd blue cuffs and lapels with white piping, the 3rd yellow cuffs and lapels with sky blue piping.

Chasseurs à Cheval Helvétiques

Helvetic Mounted Chasseurs. Created 18 April 1803 with disbanded Swiss hussars, one company strong, incorporated into 19th Chasseurs à cheval on 21 April 1804.

Uniform: green dolman with red cuffs and collar,

yellow cords; brass buttons; green breeches piped yellow; black shako with red wing edged yellow, green, red and yellow plume and cockade.

Régiments Suisses

Swiss Regiments. On 27 September 1803, France entered into another agreement with the Swiss Cantons to take into its service four regiments of Swiss soldiers, each regiment to have four battalions, each battalion to be of a thousand men for a total of 16,000. There was initially no hurry to recruit and form these units but as war with Austria, Russia and Prussia loomed, orders were given to form the units.

The 1st Regiment was formed 15 March 1805; 2nd, 3rd and 4th formed 10 October 1806. A provisional battalion was created in Spain from detached companies of the four regiments. A Swiss artillery company raised in April 1803 was attached to the 1st regiment on 1 April 1806 but actually served in Cherbourg. The three other regiments also each had an artillery company attached from 10 December 1811; regiments disbanded 1815.

Uniform: red coat, white turnbacks, regimental facing colour on collar, cuffs and lapels, regimental piping edging collar, cuffs, lapels and pockets; brass buttons; white waistcoat and breeches; shako for fusiliers and voltigeurs, bearskin cap for grenadiers.

1st: yellow collar, cuffs and lapels, sky blue piping.
2nd: blue collar, cuffs and lapels, yellow piping.
3rd: black collar, cuffs and lapels, white piping.
4th: sky blue collar, cuffs and lapels, black piping.

The artillery companies had: blue coat, regimental facings with red piping, blue cuff flaps piped red, white turnbacks with red grenade; brass buttons; shako with brass crowned eagle plate, red band, cords and pompon.

Drummers: 1st Regiment, blue coat, yellow piped sky blue collar, cuffs, cuff flaps and lapels, white turnbacks, yellow lace edging facings. 2nd Regiment, blue coat, blue collar, cuffs, cuff flaps and lapels, white turnbacks, yellow lace edging facings. 3rd, same coat as regiment with white wings edged all around with black lace. 4th, blue coat with blue cuff flaps, sky blue collar, cuffs and lapels, tricolour lace edging facings and chevrons on sleeves.

From January 1812, the basic coat and facing colours remained the same but there were changes to the piping colours. The 1st regiment had the collar, lapels and cuffs piped red, the pocket flaps piped white, shoulder straps piped yellow. The 2nd had the collar, lapels and cuffs piped red, the pocket flaps piped blue, shoulder straps piped blue. The 3rd had the collar, lapels and cuffs piped red, the pocket flaps piped white, shoulder straps piped black. The 4th had the collar, lapels and cuffs piped red, the pocket flaps piped sky blue, shoulder straps piped sky blue. Drummers had the single-breasted green coatee with Imperial livery lace.

Bataillon Valaisan

The Valais, now a Swiss Canton, was an independent republic and, on 8 October 1805, following an agreement between France and the Valais, a Valais Battalion was raised for French service. Following the incorporation of the Valais into the French Empire on 12 September 1810, the Valais Battalion was disbanded and incorporated into the 11th Light Infantry at Wesel on 16 September 1811.

Uniform: red coat, white collar, cuffs, lapels and turnbacks; brass buttons; white waistcoat and breeches; fusiliers had red piped white shoulder straps; grenadiers had white epaulettes, red shako cords, bands and plumes. Drummers: blue coat, white piped red collar, cuffs, cuff flaps, lapels and turnbacks, yellow and blue lace in up-pointed chevrons on sleeves.

Bataillon de Neuchâtel

The principality of Neuchâtel, now part of Switzerland, was granted by the Emperor to Marshal Berthier in 1806. On 11 May 1807, the 'Battalion of the Prince of Neuchâtel' was created; a company of artillery (32 gunners, 16 sappers and 16 train drivers) was attached from 27 August 1808; served in Spain and in Russia; disbanded on 1 June 1814.

Uniform: the infantry had yellow-buff coatee, scarlet collar, cuffs, square lapels and turnbacks, yellow-buff piping, vertical pockets; pewter buttons; white waistcoat and breeches; black shako with white metal eagle and chin scales. Fusiliers had white epaulettes, buffs stars on turnbacks, white shako cords and pompon. Voltigeurs had green epaulettes, green bugle horns on turnbacks, green shako cords and plumes. Grenadiers had red epaulettes, buff grenades on turnbacks, plain tall bearskin cap worn without

cords, plumes or plate for full dress; shako with red cords and plumes otherwise; buff forage cap; beige greatcoat. Sappers had red epaulettes with white crescent, bearskin cap with red plumes and cords but no plate.

Drummers had, before 1812, blue coatee with red collar, cuffs, lapels and turnbacks; blue and yellow lace edging facings and turnbacks and on up-pointed chevrons on sleeves; pewter buttons. White facings are also mentioned. From 1812, single-breasted green coatee with Imperial livery lace.

Gunners had blue coatee, blue piped yellow lapels, cuff flaps and turnbacks, yellow-buff collar and cuffs, red epaulettes; pewter buttons; blue waistcoat and breeches; black shako with brass diamond plate, red cords and plume. Train drivers had the same but light blue-grey cuffs; buff breeches and black boots. Sappers had blue coatee, blue piped red collar, cuffs and cuff flaps, yellow-buff piped red lapels and turnbacks, red epaulettes; pewter buttons; blue waistcoat and breeches; shako as gunners.

Officers for infantry, artillery and sappers had long-tailed coats, silver metal and cords.

Italy

Légion Piédmontaise, Légion du Midi

Piedmontese Legion. Created 18 May 1803; renamed Midi Legion in 1804; two battalions reduced to one battalion in November 1808; incorporated into the 82nd Line (25 May 1811) and the 11th and 31st Light (11 August 1811).

Uniform: brown coat, sky blue collar, cuffs and lapels, white turnbacks; brass buttons; white waistcoat and breeches. Grenadiers had red epaulettes and bearskin cap with brass plate, red cords and plume; Chasseurs had green epaulettes, shako with green and yellow plume; Fusiliers first had a greyish leather helmet with brass crest, black pompon and brush but no mane, greyish visor, brass chin scales; green epaulettes with yellow crescent; later the shako and brown piped sky blue shoulder straps. Drummers: same as the men with yellow lace with sky blue (?) lines edging collar and lapels and as chevrons on each sleeve; brass drum with blue hoops.

Tirailleurs du Pô

Sharpshooters of the Pô. Created 20 August 1803; incorporated into 11th Light in 1811.

Uniform: light infantry style blue coatee with blue piped white collar, red piped white collar, pointed lapels, pointed cuffs and turnbacks, red epaulettes; pewter buttons; white waistcoat; blue pantaloons;

black light infantry gaiters edged red; hat with falling red plume; white accoutrements. From 1806, blue coatee with blue collar and pointed lapels, white cuffs, cuff flaps, piping and turnbacks; pewter buttons; shako with white metal diamond plate, white cords and green plume.

Dragons Toscans

Tuscan Dragoons. Created 7 January 1808; became 28th Chasseurs à cheval on 29 May 1808.

Uniform: completely green coatee and trousers, amaranth piping edging collar, pointed cuffs, lapels and turnbacks; amaranth epaulettes; amaranth stripes on trousers.

Gardes D'Honneur de Turin, de Florence

Companies of Guards of Honour created by Napoleon on 1 April 1809, one in Torino and one in Florence, as horse guards for his sisters, princess Caroline Borghese in Torino and Elisa, Grand Duchess of Tuscany. Although not officially part of the Imperial Guard, their duties were much the same. The Florentine company served in the Russian campaign and remnants disbanded on 16 July 1813. The Torino company was disbanded on 1 May 1814.

Uniform for both companies in 1809: scarlet long-tailed coat, blue collar, cuffs and lapels, vertical pockets, silver aiguillettes and epaulettes; silver buttons; white waistcoat and breeches; long black boots; bicorn hat laced silver; blue housings laced silver. Officers had silver oak leaf embroidery 2 cm wide edging collar, cuffs, lapels and pocket flaps; NCOs had embroidery on collar, cuffs and pocket flaps. Hat later replaced by a scarlet shako with silver eagle plate, blue embroidered silver top and bottom band and upside down 'v' at sides, silver cords, silver pompon and tall red plume.

Compagnies de Sbires, de Police

Armed constabulary unit raised in Tuscany on 19 May 1809; four companies; renamed Police Companies in June 1809. Other companies raised in Rome on 31 July 1811.

Uniform: grey single-breasted coatee with grey collar and cuffs; pewter buttons; grey waistcoat and pantaloons; black half gaiters; round hat with upturned brim on left side with white cockade loop and grey pompon.

Régiment de la Méditérranée

Mediterranean Regiment. Formed 27 January 1810 with refractory conscripts in northern Italy and Corsican Chasseurs; became 35th Chasseurs à pied 20

Chef de bataillon P.J. Blanc, Valaisan Battalion (Swiss), c. 1807-1811. Print after portrait.

September 1812.

Uniform: same as the French light infantry.

Vétérans Romains

Company of Roman Veterans created 30 April 1810; incorporated with two companies of Ligurian Veterans into the 9th Imperial Veteran's (continued on p. 129) Battalion on 25 August 1810.

Uniform: sky blue coatee with red piped white collar and cuffs, white square lapels to the waist, white cuff flaps, sky blue piped white shoulder straps; pewter buttons; white breeches and long gaiters; shako with red top band and pompon, brass plate and chin scales. Later same as French veterans.

Bataillon de Chasseurs-Flaqueurs (Elba)

Flankers-Chasseurs Battalion. Four-company unit formed by Napoleon at Elba from a battalion of the 35th Chasseurs (ex-Régiment de la Méditérranée) during 1814. Went to France with Napoleon, landing at Golfe-Juan on 1 March 1815 and incorporated into 1st Voltigeurs of the Young Guard as its 2nd battalion on 8 April.

Capt. De Brun, Neuchâtel Battalion (Swiss), c. 1807-1814. Print after portrait by Louis Boily.

Uniform: same as French light infantry but Napoleon wanted to change it. On 2 April 1815, he asked that the first three companies have green uniforms and the fourth blue. It seems however that, because of supply difficulties, the light infantry uniform continued to be used.

Germans

Régiment la Tour D'Auvergne

La Tour d'Auvergne Regiment. Created 30 September 1805; three light infantry battalions; to be recruited from Germans 'and other foreigners'; became '1er régiment étranger' (1st Foreign Regiment) on 3 August 1811; disbanded 25 November 1813.

Uniform: light infantry style green coatee with green lapels, cuffs and turnbacks, scarlet collar and cuff flaps, white piping edging facings, white epaulettes; pewter buttons; white waistcoat, green pantaloons; shako with brass plate and chin scales, white cords, green plume. Carabiniers, red shako cords, top band and plume; red epaulettes.

Régiment D'Isembourg

Isembourg Regiment. Created 1 November 1805; to be recruited solely from Germans; became '2e régiment étranger' (2nd Foreign Regiment) on 3 August 1811; disbanded 25 November 1813.

Uniform: light infantry style sky blue coatee with sky blue lapels, pointed cuffs and turnbacks, yellow collar, white piping; pewter buttons; sky blue waistcoat and pantaloons; black half gaiter; shako with brass plate and chin scales. Fusiliers had sky blue piped white shoulder straps, white cords and sky blue pompon with white centre. Voltigeurs, green epaulettes with yellow crescent, green cords, green feather tipped yellow. Grenadiers, red epaulettes, bearskin cap with white cords and red plume. Drummers: as above with sky blue wings edged with white lace.

Régiment de Prusse

Prussian Regiment. Created 13 November 1806; recruited among former soldiers of the Prussian army; became '4e régiment étranger' (4th Foreign Regiment) on 3 August 1811; disbanded 25 November 1813.

Uniform: initially green somewhat Prussian cut coatee with red square lapels, cuffs, collar and turnbacks, plain green shoulder straps; brass buttons; green breeches; black gaiters edged yellow; French shako with brass plate with white cords and plume for fusilier, red for grenadier, yellow for voltigeur. From c. 1810: light infantry style green coatee with green pointed lapels and cuffs, scarlet collar, turnbacks and piping; pewter buttons; green waistcoat and pantaloons; shako. Drummers c. 1807: white coatee, red collar, cuffs, lapels, shoulder straps, wings and probably turnbacks, red and white lace edging facings and wings; brass buttons; green breeches; shako with brass plaque, white cords and plume; brass drum with red and yellow hoops.

Régiment de Westphalie

Westphalia Regiment. Light infantry unit created 11 December 1806; four battalions, each of six companies; recruited from former Prussian soldiers; incorporated into the Hanoverian Legion 30 September 1809.

Uniform: 'white uniform, red cuffs and collar; the coat and the headdress, the armament and the accoutrements will be in the Prussian infantry style and we will use for that purpose anything that can be found in the [Prussian] stores' decreed Napoleon. Arms and accoutrements were Prussian taken at Jena.

Foreign troops in French service, Russia, summer of 1812.

Napoleon's Imperial armies included a large number of foreign units representing many nationalities. In 1812, most were assembled in Poland and, in June, crossed the Niemen River into Russia. The march of the Grande Armée's 420,000 men into the interior of Russia was punctuated by a number of relatively small engagements and a multitude of skirmishes with the retreating Russians. The plate opposite shows members of units in Marshal Oudinot's Second Army Corps skirmishing in the summer of 1812.

All four Swiss regiments were part of the corps and they wore the traditional red coatee of Swiss regiments in French service, with blue facings for the 2nd Regiment (bottom) according to the latest regulation issued in January 1812. The Voltigeurs of the regiment had yellow epaulettes, collar, shako band, pompon and sabre knot. Grey pantaloons with a red stripe were worn by this, and many other, infantry units in Russia.

The 2nd Corps included the 3rd Croat Provisional Regiment (top left), one of three regiments from Croatia assembled for 'provisional' active duty from late 1811. They were uniformed in green and yellow uniforms of the old light infantry cut and just missed the new 1812 regulation style. However, green trousers with yellow stripes were worn into

Russia. The elite Carabiniers were distinguished by red epaulettes, shako bands, plume and sabre knot.

The brown-clad 3rd line regiment of the Portuguese Legion (top right) also marched into Russia as part of Oudinot's 2nd Corps. They had a distinct Portuguese shako with raised front, said to have inspired the British 'Belgic' shako, and wore a coatee with lapels that squared off just above the waist. Pantaloons were white with red piping and stripes. Grenadiers had red plume, cords, epaulettes and sabre knot. Painting by Christa Hook.

Top left.
Private, Albanian Regiment (Albanian and Greek), c. 1808-1813. Watercolour by Herbert Knötel. John Elting, Cornwall, USA.

Top right.
Carabinier officer, Irish Legion, c, 1810. Print after Vernet.

Serezaner (Croat), c. 1809-1814. These mountain patrol troops wore a mixture of uniform and Balkans costume. Watercolour by Herbert Knötel. John Elting, Cornwall, USA.

Officer, Piedmontese (or Midi) Legion, c. 1807-1811. Watercolour by Herbert Knötel. John Elting, Cornwall, USA.

Bataillon Septinsulaire

Septinsular Battalion. The Ionian islands were often called the 'seven islands' or 'septinsulaire' by the French. Raised 1807 as a light infantry battalion with the men of a former Venetian regiment; served on Dalmatian coast and Ionian islands; disbanded 1814.

Uniform: possibly a blue coatee with blue lapels, cuffs and lining, sky blue collar and cuff flaps, sky blue piping; pewter buttons; blue waistcoat and trousers; short black gaiters; light infantry shako with brass plate. However, research in the archives by the late Roger Forthoffer revealed only blue and red cloth for this unit.

Other Septinsulaires Corps

Two companies of Septinsular Artillery (Artillerie septinsulaire) raised 1 January 1808; a Company of Ionian Sappers; a Company of Veterans; a Company of Septinsular Gendarmerie. Served on Dalmatian coast and Ionian islands. All were disbanded in 1814.

Uniform: all reportedly were organized, armed and uniformed as the French corps. However, the

Gendarmerie at Corfu in 1812 had a blue single-breasted coatee with red collar, cuffs, piping and turnbacks, blue piped red cuff flaps and shoulder straps; brass buttons; buff waistcoat and breeches; black long gaiters; also blue pantaloons and short black gaiters; black shako with brass plate and chin scales, red pompon; white infantry accoutrements; musket and bayonet, short sabre and a pair of pistols carried in front on a white waist belt with open holsters. Drummers had the same with white lace edging the collar and cuffs.

Régiment Albanais

Albanian Regiment. Was in Russian pay, passed into French service in 1807; reorganized on 1 July 1809 into six battalions in Corfu and the Ionian islands with refugee Albanians and some Greeks which formed a battalion of Greek Foot Chasseurs (Bataillon de chasseurs à pied grecs) within the regiment; the men served as volunteers and could leave the service as they pleased; detachments on Ionian islands attacked by British in October 1809 surrendered without a fight;

discipline was somewhat lax but they made good partisans; reduced to two battalions on 6 November 1813; passed into British service following the French evacuation of Corfu in June 1814.

Uniform: the men could not bear adopting a military uniform and kept wearing their regional costumes. Basically an ample 'Greek' shirt fastened with a waist belt, a sleeveless jacket, breeches and stockings or leggings, a cloak of coarse cloth, a low dark red cap. They were armed with musket, sabre and often a brace of pistols as well. A small cartridge box was on the waist belt.

Chasseurs d'Illyrie

Illyrian Chasseurs. Following the Treaty of Vienna of October 1809, Croatia and Slovenia became part of the French Empire. The French found there six Croat border regiments named after different localities. These units grouped able-bodied men in the border area which were kept ready to be mobilized against 'Turkish' raiders in Bosnia. They were reorganized by the French into six regiments of 'Chasseurs d'Illyrie' in May 1810; two battalions of 240 men each divided into six companies, plus a third reserve battalion called up in war time; disbanded November 1813.

Uniform: initially continued to wear the brown Austrian uniform from 1809 with regimental facings listed below. On 22 May 1810, uniform ordered to be blue coatee with collar, cuffs and turnbacks of regimental colour; pewter buttons; white waistcoat; blue trousers; Hungarian-style boots; French shako; beige greatcoat. Attempts to dye the Austrian coatees blue ended up in vaguely black coatees which were allowed until blue could be procured. The facings were red for the 1st Illyrian Chasseurs (former Lika Regiment), crimson for the 2nd (former Ottochatz), yellow for the 3rd (Ogulin), violet changed to orange in June for the 4th (Sluin), sky blue for the 5th (1st Banat), and green for the 6th (2nd Banat).

From late 1811 and early 1812, light infantry style green coatee, green pointed lapels, yellow collar, pointed cuffs, turnbacks and lapel piping; pewter buttons; green waistcoat; green pantaloons; black half gaiters edged yellow; shako with white metal plate and chin scales; company pompons and epaulettes; green forage cap piped in the regimental colour. For distinction, each regiment often had a pointed collar patch of the regimental colour.

Serezaner

Also termed Serrigiani or Sereschaner. Croatian sedentary mountain border guard militia, often mounted. The men were not paid when called on service but served only in their home area and were exempt from enlistment in the Illyrian Chasseurs.

Uniform: there was no strict military dress per say but they appear to have worn the brown of the Austrian border troops; the men being allowed some money for their clothing and equipment. A mounted Serezaner would have a brown jacket with red collar and cuffs; pewter buttons; brown pelisse with red edging and cords; blueish or whitish trousers with red stripe and red Hungarian knots; red cape lined white; fur busby with red bag. Armed with a long barreled musket, a kandjar knife and a pair of pistols; Turkish style saddlery.

Régiment d'Illyrie

Illyrian Regiment. Created 16 November 1810; regular regiment of five battalions recruited in Croatia; a third of the officers were French and Belgians; had recruiting difficulties, other nationalities allowed into it notably Lithuanians; posted in Kosvno; down to one battalion in early 1813; evacuated to France and disbanded 17 November 1813.

Uniform: same as French light infantry but, the Emperor wished the coatee to have in addition, [scarlet?] wings edged with white. The unit is said to have been in rags by November 1813, most men lacking shoes and unable to march.

Régiments Provisoires Croates

Croatian Provisional Regiments. Three provisional regiments of two battalions each called up on active duty in September and October 1811 from the 1st battalions of the six border 'Illyrian Chasseurs' and appear to have dissolved in the retreat from Russia; four provisional regiments mobilized in 1813 for active duty but 2nd Regiment mutinied and others proved unreliable; disbanded late 1813.

Uniform: the three units activated in the fall of 1811 had the green light infantry uniform described above for the Chasseurs Illyriens but also had yellow waistcoats, green pantaloons with yellow stripe. The four 1813 units were clothed with Austrian uniforms found in stores: brown single-breasted coatee with yellow collar, pointed cuffs, turnbacks and piping in front; white metal buttons; brown trousers; Hungarian-style ankle boots; black Austrian shako with front and back visors, tricolour cockade with white cockade loop.

Hussards Croates

Croatian Hussars. Regiment created 23 February 1813 as four squadrons (two regiments were planned but one was actually raised); establishment raised to six squadrons totaling 1584 on 3 March; 200 took part in successful defense of Karlstadt against Bosnian Turks; strength was 657 in June and some French personnel allowed in to raise effective strength; went to France in October and disbanded 1276 strong in Lyon on 25 November 1813.

Uniform: sky blue dolman, buff collar and cuffs; light grey-blue pelisse edged with black lambskin; pewter buttons; white cords; crimson and white sash; light grey-blue breeches with white cords; hussar boots edged white; pantaloons strapped with black leather; black shako with white metal diamond plate and chin scales, pompon of squadron colour; white belts; black leather sabretache with silver crowned eagle and letters 'I H C' (1er Hussards Croates) below; light grey-blue cloak; sheepskin housingsedged buff, light grey-blue valise.

Pionniers Croates

Battalion of Croatian Pioneers. Raised late 1813 from personnel of disbanded Croatian Hussars; sent to Bourges; disbanded 1814.

Uniform: same as 'Pionniers Blancs'.

Pandours de Dalmatie

Dalmatian Pandours. Also called Pandours of Ragusa (Dubrovnik). Organized 17 March 1810; one battalion of nine companies, each company having from 36 to 48 Pandours including two drummers; guarded the south-eastern border, escorted couriers, watched 'Turkish' caravans from Bosnia; disbanded 25 November 1813.

Uniform: according to an order 17 March 1810, it was 'red dolman, laced silver, edged with sheepskin for the Pandours; red jacket; blue pantaloon; red turban; opanque.' White cloaks for private Pandours, red for non-commissioned officers. Fieffé adds that this was later altered to blue dolman, red cloak for all and a French-style shako. They were armed with 'regulation muskets, pistols, kandjars in the shape of hunting knives, cartridge box at the waist belt; sabre and pistols for the officers'. Officers were to wear the same uniform with their troops with rank badges as in the light cavalry and have hussar boots. But they were also allowed to wear the blue French-style coat with red turnbacks and red pantaloons, silver buttons and epaulettes.

Holland

Holland was absorbed into the French Empire on 9 July 1810. As a result, the 27,000 strong Dutch army was amalgamated into the French Army and adopted French uniforms. There were, however, a few distinct corps.

Officer, Isembourg Regiment (German), c. 1810. Miniature, J. Ostiguy collection, Ottawa.

Bataillons Expéditionaires des Indes

Expeditionary Battalions of the Indies. Created 6 September 1810; two Companies of Expeditionary Artillery also created in September; sent towards Java in February 1811 but part of force captured in May after a fight near Tamatave, Madagascar, others held Mahé in the Seychelles and managed to get back to Brest and incorporated into other units.

Uniform: same as French line infantry and artillery.

Régiment de Walcheren

Walcheren Regiment. Formed with refractory conscripts created 24 January 1811 to serve in Walcheren Island, off the Dutch coast; first two battalions had mostly Belgians, the 3rd Spaniards; became 131st of the Line in 1812; disbanded 1814.

Uniform: blue coat with blue piped red collar, cuffs, lapels and shoulder straps, white turnbacks; brass buttons; white waistcoat and breeches; black shako with brass diamond plate and chin scales. The 3rd 'Spanish' Battalion had a different coat: blue with blue piped yellow lapels, shoulder straps and cuff flaps, red piped yellow collar and cuffs, white turnbacks, brass buttons. Standard infantry uniform adopted from 1812.

Garde Soldée d'Amsterdam

Amsterdam Paid Guard. Created 22 October 1811; two battalions of four companies each and a squadron of cavalry; dissolved in late 1813.

Uniform: blue coat, pink collar, cuffs and lapels, pewter buttons; white waistcoat and breeches. The infantry had the same style and cut as the line infantry. The cavalry wore the same colours but the uniform was in the style of the Chasseurs à cheval.

Garde Soldée de Rotterdam

Rotterdam Paid Guard. Created 16 November 1811; one infantry company; dissolved late 1813.

Uniform: blue coat, white collar, cuffs and lapels, pewter buttons; white waistcoat and breeches in the same style and cut as the line infantry.

Bataillon de Pionniers

Pioneer Battalion. Organized with Dutch personnel in January 1814; disbanded later in the year.

Uniform: probably the same as the 'Pionniers Blancs'.

Other Nationalities

Bataillons Étrangers

Foreign Battalions. Two battalions created on 23 March 1802; 3rd battalion in 1809; recruited from various foreign deserters and used mostly for garrison and coast guard duties; disbanded 1814.

Uniform: according to Elting and Knötel, the 3rd had in c. 1810-1811 a sky blue coat, sky blue piped blue cuffs, lapels, turnbacks and shoulder straps, blue collar and cuff flaps; pewter buttons; white waistcoat and breeches; black gaiters; shako with white metal plate and chin scales, sky blue pompon.

Légion Irlandaise

Irish Legion. Created 31 August 1803; one battalion; raised to two then three in 1809 and renamed 'Régiment irlandais' but recruited from all nations; became '3e régiment étranger' (3rd Foreign Regiment) on 25 November 1811; only 65 Irishmen left by 1813; reorganized as 7th Foreign Regiment on 2 May 1815; disbanded 29 September 1815.

Uniforms: light infantry style green coatee, yellow collar, pointed cuffs, lapels, turnbacks and piping; brass buttons; white waistcoat and pantaloons; black gaiters with red (carabiniers) or green trim. Carabinier

had red shako cords and plume, red epaulettes, red grenade on turn back. Voltigeurs had green shako cords, green tipped yellow plume, green epaulettes with yellow crescent, green horn on turn back. Chasseurs had white shako cords, green plume, green piped yellow shoulder straps, green horn on turnbacks. From 1810, green piped yellow lapels, cuffs, turnbacks, yellow cuff flaps; pewter buttons; green waistcoat and breeches. Model 1812 coatee apparently issued in 1813; sky blue coatee with red collar, lapels and cuff flaps in 1814-15. Drummers: unknown, possibly as the men with white lace edging facings and yellow wings.

Guides-Interprètes de l'Armée d'Angleterre

Guides-Interpreters of the Army of England. Company of light dragoons created 3 October 1803, of 117 men including two drummers and five officers, recruited especially from Irish volunteers in Paris and Channel ports who could speak and translate English. Attached to HQ during the Boulogne episode; transferred to Poland and became part of Marshal Berthier's Guides in 1806.

Uniform: 'green coatee, red lining, scarlet lapels, cuffs and turnbacks, white hussar style buttons, white cloth waistcoat, white buttons, white breeches, American style boots, black bronzed spurs' according to the decree creating it. Bicorn laced white with red plume; green housings laced white. White accoutrements, dragoon musket and sabre.

Pionniers Blancs/Pionniers Volontaires Étrangers

White Pioneers. Regiment created 15 February 1806; two battalions of four companies each recruited from Austrian prisoners; reorganized as a Foreign Volunteer Pioneers Battalion of five companies on 1 September 1810, sixth company formed at Bourges in February 1811 and two more in September from captured followers of Schill and the Duke of Brunswick which must have made most reluctant 'volunteers'; remnants of unit incorporated into 3rd Foreign Colonial Battalion in August 1814.

Uniform: all light grey-blue single-breasted round jacket, waistcoat, pantaloons, cloth buttons, forage cap, short gaiters and greatcoat with brass buttons; bicorn hat and later shako. Privates only had tools, only NCOs were armed with dragoon musket and bayonet.

Légion Portugaise

Portuguese Legion. Created 16 January 1808 and organized from 18 May 1808 with part of disbanded

Portuguese army following Napoleon's invasion of that country in 1807. The legion had six, later five, light infantry regiments of six companies of 140 men each, two mounted chasseurs regiments of four squadrons each with two companies of 100 men each, and a short-lived battery of light artillery. Augmented in 1809 by a half-brigade of elite companies; reduced to three infantry regiments and one of mounted chasseurs on 2 May 1811; disbanded November 1813.

Uniform: brown coatee, red piped white collar, cuffs, square lapels and turnbacks (also shown white); pewter buttons; white waistcoat; brown trousers with red piping and red stripe to each side, white in summer; black Portuguese felt shako with high front (somewhat like the British 'Belgic' shako), low brass plate coming to a point at centre front bearing regimental number; red epaulettes, shako plume, cords and brass grenade plate for grenadiers; green epaulettes with yellow crescent, green shako cords, yellow over red plume and brass bugle horn badge for chasseurs. Many variations to the above. White undress jacket with red collar and cuffs; brown fatigue cap; beige greatcoat. Drummers had white lace edging the facings and chevrons on the sleeves.

Mounted chasseurs had the same but with red wings; grey-blue cavalry trousers with red stripe; black boots; black leather helmet with black caterpillar crest, red plume; white sheepskin housings edged red. Trumpeters had a coatee of reversed colours, yellow wings laced and fringed white; white helmet plume. From 1812, the men had a brown single-breasted coatee, French Chasseurs à cheval cut, with red collar, pointed cuffs, turnbacks and piping; pewter buttons; brown trousers breeches laced white; brown overalls with red stripe; French shako with white cords and green pompon; busby with red bag piped white for elite company.

Officers had gold metal and lace and a red sash around the waist until 1812, silver metal and lace thereafter, and no sash.

Pionniers Portugais
Portuguese Pioneers. Battalion raised in 1812; same establishment as French pioneer battalions; disbanded April 1814.

Uniform: same as 'Pionniers Blancs' battalions.

Régiment Joseph-Napoléon
Joseph-Napoléon Regiment. Raised 13 February 1809 in Spain; four battalions, reduced to two in 1813; disbanded 25 November 1813.

Uniform: white coat, light green collar, cuffs, lapels

Chasseur, Portuguese Legion, 1810. Cavalry wearing the legion's distinctive helmet and white cloaks are in the background. Print after Vernet.

and turnbacks; brass buttons; white waistcoat and breeches; shako with brass eagle plate.

Régiment de Catalogne
Catalan Regiment. Created in Spain on 2 February 1811; three battalions to have 2558 officers and men; regiment was completing its organization when Wellington's victory at Salamanca (12 July 1812) caused its dissolution.

Uniform: white coat, sky blue collar, cuffs and lapels; brass buttons; white waistcoat and breeches; shako with brass eagle plate.

Sapeurs Espagnols
Spanish Sappers. Battalion formed 18 February 1811; similar establishment as French; became 8th Sapper Battalion in 1812; remnants become Company of Spanish Sappers in December 1813; disbanded May 1814.

Uniform: same as French sappers.

Pionniers, Ouvriers Espagnols

Battalion of Spanish Pioneers and two Companies of Spanish Artisans. Formed in Holland from Spanish P.O.W.s 10 March 1812; disbanded 25 November 1813; reorganized as Regiment of Spanish Pioneers (Régiment de pionniers espagnols) on 24 December 1813; disbanded 17 April 1814.

Uniform: grey round jacket with blue collar, cuffs and lapels, yellow piping; grey greatcoat. Armed only with a hanger and a pioneer's tool.

Bataillons de Pionniers Espagnols

Two Spanish Pioneer Battalions formed in January 1814 with remnants of King Joseph's Spanish army which had fled to France; disbanded 1st and 6 August 1814.

Uniform: probably the all light grey-blue dress of the 'Pionniers Blancs' if they received one.

Other Spanish Units

There were also some contra-guerrilla units in French pay raised especially in Catalonia among Miquelets mountaineers. They generally wore a brown round jacket and trousers with red collar, cuffs, stripes and sashes, round hat with tricolour cockade. Marshal Suchet raised the 'Guides Catalans' in 1810 which had 50 mounted and 100 infantrymen for escorts. They had a blue coatee, single breasted, blue pointed cuffs and turnbacks, medium green collar, yellow piping in front, at cuffs, collar and turnbacks; pewter buttons; white waistcoat and breeches; plain bicorn; boots and sabres for mounted men, gaiters and muskets for infantry. In 1813, the Independent Company of Alava Infantry was formed by pro-French Spaniards. The uniform was in the French 1812 style but brown coatee with red collar, cuffs, lapels and turnbacks; pewter buttons; brown trousers; shako.

Régiment Lithuanien

Lithuanian Regiment. Infantry regiment created 20 September 1812; had Polish and French officers; dissolved in late 1813.

Uniform: blue kurta, yellow collar, pointed cuffs, lapels and turnbacks; white metal buttons; blue pantaloons with yellow stripe; czapska with blue crown, yellow piping and band, white metal sunrise plate with brass badge (Lithuania's national insignia: an armed horseman), white cockade with white metal Polish cross, company pompon. Grenadier in 1813 had bearskin cap, uniform completely blue with yellow lace edging collar, cuffs, lapels; white epaulettes; blue pantaloons with white stripe.

Gendarmes Lithuaniens

Lithuanian Gendarmes. Organised in 1812 during the invasion of Russia to keep some law and order along the French lines of communications; proved to be excellent cavalry and charged at Borodino; retreated with French Army in Russia and about 200 incorporated into 1st Polish Lancers in 1813.

Uniform: blue single-breasted coatee with red cuffs, collar, turnbacks and piping in front, white trefoils and aiguillette; pewter buttons; white or blue breeches; high boots; white belts; bicorn edged with white lace; blue housings laced white with white grenade; red over white lance pennon.

Foreign Regiments of 1815

Back in Paris from Elba, Napoleon disbanded the Swiss troops on 2 April 1815 and the next day suggested the reorganization of Foreign troops into five regiments, each of three battalions. The decrees of 11 and 25 April and of 20 May created eight: 1st (Piedmontese, organized at Châlon-sur-Soane); 2nd (Swiss, Vitry), 3rd (Polish, at Reims), 4th (German, at Tours), 5th (Belgian, at Amiens), 6th (Spanish and Portuguese, at Lorient from the former 'Regiment Colonial Étranger'); 7th (Irish, at Montreuil-sur-Mer); 8th (Italian, at Aix). Only the 2nd sufficiently organized to follow the army in Belgium, others partly raised and equipped did garrison service; disbanded 6 September 1825.

Uniforms: Napoleon felt that each should have its traditional colour, 'the Piedmontese (1st) in blue which I suppose to be the colour of the Piedmontese uniform so as to use the volunteers in the dress in which they will arrive' and the Swiss (2nd) in red, the Poles (3rd) in Polish style dress. The 6th regiment was to have a 'white uniform'. The 7th had the uniform of the old 'Legion Irlandaise' (see notice on that corps). The 8th was to have 'green, scarlet facings'.

Bibliography

Books

Blondiau, Christian, *Aigles et shakos du Premier Empire*, Paris, 1980. Invaluable reference work on headdress and shako plates.

Bory, Jean-René, *Régiments suisses au service de France (1800-1814)*, Fribourg, 1975.

Brosse, Jacques and Henri Lachouque, *Uniformes et costumes du 1er Empire*, Paris, 1972. Many period prints and painting in colour.

Bulletin des lois. The legislative periodical of the French National Assembly. Contains many military decrees with uniform descriptions, especially during the Consulate.

Chartrand, René, *Napoleon's Overseas Army*, London, 1989 and Napoleon's *Sea-Soldiers*, London, 1990. More data and colour reconstructions by Francis Back on these neglected but no less interesting and colourful units of Napoleon's forces.

Chuquet, Arthur, *Ordres et apostilles de Napoléon*, Paris, 1911-1912, 4 Vols.

Constant, Louis, *Mémoires de Constant, premier valet de chambre de l'Empéreur sur la vie privée de Napoléon, sa famille et sa cour*. Many reprints. We have used the 1969 Geneva edition. The source for Napoleon's private habits, taste and daily routines from the valet who helped him put on his uniform every morning.

Correspondance de Napoléon 1er..., Paris, 1858-1870, 32 Vols. and *Correspondance militaire de Napoléon 1er...*, Paris, 1876, 5 Vols. The ultimate printed sources on Napoleon, many good documents on army organization and postings, relatively few on uniforms, arms and equipment.

Delpierre, Madeleine, 'Les costume de cour et les uniformes civils du premier empire', *Bulletin du Musée Carnavalet*, Nov. 1958. The best study on uniforms of high-ranking government officials.

Fieffé, Eugène, *Histoire des troupes étrangères au service de France...*, Paris, 1854, 2 Vols. Still the classic study on foreign units.

Elting, John R., *Napoleonic Uniforms*, New York, 1993, 2 Vols. A superb luxury edition in colour of hundreds of watercolours by the acclaimed German illustrator Herbert Knötel, possibly the only work showing nearly all units in the Imperial army.

Elting, John R., *Swords around a throne*, New York, 1989. The most complete work in English on the Grande Armée, told with considerable incisive wit.

Glasser, Otto von, *Costumes militaires: catalogue des principales suites de costumes militaires français...*, Paris, 1900. The outstanding bibliography of French military prints.

Journal Militaire. Periodical publication containing orders and instructions to the armed forces. Superlative source for uniform decrees which we have constantly used in this book. But it should be used with caution and verified against other sources.

Haythornthwaite, Philip J., *The Napoleonic Source Book*, London, 1990. Excellent and essential work covering the whole period and the main countries involved. Much useful data on uniforms, armament, etc.

Haythornthwaite, Philip J., *Napoleon's Line Infantry*, London, 1983, *Napoleon's Light Infantry*, London, 1983, *Napoleon's Specialist Troops*, London, 1988. Good studies of uniforms, arms, equipment and abstract of service for many units.

Malibran, H., *Guide à l'usage des artistes et costumiers contenant la description des uniformes l'Armée française de 1780 à 1848*, Paris, 1904. One of the most useful standard works describing uniforms. No illustrations but a book of patterns was published to accompany the 'Guide' about 1907.

Marbot, Marcellin, *Mémoires...*, Paris, 1892, 3 Vols. Real memoirs that read like a novel! Marbot was ADC to several marshals and gives a fine view of the period and its actors. Useful remarks on uniforms and supplies.

Margérand, J., *Armement et équipement de l'infanterie française du XVIe au XXe siècle*, Paris, 1945.

Morvan, Jean, *Le soldat impérial, 1800-1814*, Paris,

1904, 2 Vols. The ultimate work if you wish to know about the army's supply shortages.

Lachouque, Henri and Anne S.K. Brown, *The Anatomy of Glory: Napoleon's Imperial Guard*, Brown University, Providence, R.I., 1961, 2nd edition 1962, reprinted. A classic work, for both the text and for the superb illustrations.

Lienhart, Dr. and René Humbert, *Les uniformes de l'Armée française depuis 1690 jusqu'à nos jours*, Leipzig, 1897-1902, 5 Vols. A standard source for copious descriptions with many schematic plates. Vol. 5 on allied troops to be used with caution.

Pétard, Michel, *Équipements militaires de 1600 à 1870*, Olonne-sur-mer, France, 10 Vols., 1984-1994. Vol. 3 deals with the 1789-1803 period, vols. 4 and 5 with the 1804-1815 period. As definitive a study as is ever likely to be made on this subject. Superlative with hundreds of fine drawings and extracts from contemporary texts.

Riehn, Richard K., *The French Imperial Army: the Campaigns of 1813-1814 and Waterloo*, Woodhaven, N.Y., 1959, and *The French Infantry and Artillery*, 1795-1812, Queens, N.Y., 1963. These two 'Helenic Uniform Guides' booklets are an outstanding summary of French Napoleonic uniforms.

Willing, Paul, *Napoléon et ses soldats; l'apogée de la gloire, 1804-1809*, Paris, 1983. Hundreds of photos of paintings and objects in France's two 'Musée de l'Armée'. A treat!

Windrow, Martin and Gerry Embleton, *Military Dress of the Peninsular War*, London, 1974. Excellent B&W illustrations of artefacts and paintings, Embleton's colour figures among best ever produced.

Plate Books and Print Series

Béllangé, Hippolyte, *Collection de types de tous les corps et des uniformes militaires de la république et de l'empire*, Paris, 1844. Béllangé's plates and line drawings illustrated numerous books of the period.

Berka and Zimner, *L'Armée française*, Prague, c.1810.

Charlet, Nicolas-Toussaint, *Costumes militaires français*, Paris, 1818.

Faber du Faur, Christian G. de, published over 100 lithographs from his sketches of the 1812 Russian campaign in Stuttgart, 1831-1843. Excellent source on campaign dress and miseries of retreat from Russia.

Forthoffer, Roger, *Fiches documentaires*. Excellent plate series published in Romans, France, from the 1960s to the early 1980s. Covered not only French but all armies from 1792-1815.

JOB (Jacques Onfroy de Bréville), *Tenues des troupes de France*, Paris, c. 1900-1913. JOB also illustrated many historical works, notably luxury children's books such as *Bonaparte* and *Napoléon* in the early 1900s and later *La vieille garde impériale*, Tours, 1929. Many are reproduced in this book.

Girbal, Jack and Hourtoule, René, *Soldats et uniformes du premier empire*. Series of plates published in France from the late 1960s to the early 1980s. Good synthesis of available sources, especially useful for the more obscure units.

Hoffman, Nicolaus. Published individual prints of French Army from c. 1780 to c. 1807. Very rare and fine.

Marbot, Alfred de. Prints on the French Napoleonic army published in Paris during the 1840s.

Martinet, Pierre, *Troupes françaises*, Paris, 296 coloured plates published from 1807 to 1815. One of the main primary sources, sometimes the only one for lesser known units and details.

Rigo [Albert Rigondeau], *Le Plumet*. Series of uniform prints published from the 1960s usually based on excellent data from archival sources.

Rousselot, Lucien, *L'Armée française: ses uniformes, son armement, ses équipements*. Series published in Paris from the 1940s to the 1970s. The one outstanding, obligatory modern source on Napoleonic uniforms one must consult. Some have recently been translated and republished in English.

Suhr, Christoph. Print series published in Hamburg showing over 500 uniforms of c. 1807-1814, very few originals known. Some re-drawn facsimiles later published as the 'Manuscrit du bourgeois de Hambourg' but original prints are much better.

Vernet, Horace and Eugène Lami, *Collection des uniformes des armées françaises de 1791-1814*, Paris, 1822. A primary source.

Weiland, C.F., *Darstellung der K.K. Französischen Armee und ihrer Alliren*, Weimar, 1807-1808. A primary source.

Post card series should also be mentioned as they are small prints and can be important sources. The most extensive was published by Commandant Eugène-Louis Bucquois from 1911 to the 1950s titled *Les Uniformes du Premier Empire*, republished in book form in the 1980s. Much less numerous but quite important sources are the postcards showing the mannequins with original uniforms published by the two Musée de l'Armée in France.

Napoleonic Wars Directory

This directory is a comprehensive guide for Napoleonic re-enactors, historians, art collectors, modellers and wargamers.

Napoleonic Re-enactment Groups

The umbrella organisation for many of the Napoleonic re-enactment groups in Britain is the long established Napoleonic Association organising events not only in this country but throughout Europe. Over the years the NA has grown from a purely re-enactment organisation to incorporate research and wargaming sections and members also receive the magazine, *First Empire*. For details write to the Chairman, Mike Freeman, 5 Thingwall Drive, Irby, Wirral, Merseyside L61 3XN.

Winners of *Military Illustrated's* Best Re-enactment Group award in 1995, the 12th Light Dragoons are one of Britain's finest living history groups. The 12th have high standards of authenticity and horsemanship and pride themselves on maintaining the spirit of the original regiment they proudly base themselves upon. Contact Martin Render, Shepherd's Cottage, Fernhill, Glemsford, Suffolk, CO10 7PR for details.

Another fine cavalry unit is the 15th King's Light Dragoons (Hussars) who are also very exacting in their standards. The 15th can be contacted through Neil Leonard, Rose Cottage, Caledonia, Winlaton, Tyne & Wear, NE21 6AX.

The 3rd Battalion 1st Foot Guards portray the elite troops who fought under Wellington through the Peninsula and Waterloo campaigns. The unit is run by Waterloo expert Derek Saunders who can be contacted at the Waterloo Museum, Crow Hill, Broadstairs, Kent, CT10 lHN.

The 2nd Queen's Regiment of Foot recreates the 2nd Foot during the early years of the Peninsular War. Contact G. Brown, 18 Lilac Close, Bellfields Estate, Guildford, Surrey, GUl lPB.

The 42nd Royal Highland Regiment was formed over a decade ago and its events include displays at Fort Amherst, Chatham, Kent, Britain's premier Napoleonic fort. Contact R. Prisley, 37 Byron Road, Gillingham, Kent ME7 5QH.

The 68th (Durham) Light Infantry has become widely renowned for its painstaking authenticity and recreates one of the fine regiments that fought in the Peninsula. Contact Tony Parker, 213 Bishopton Road West, Fairfield, Stockton, Cleveland, TSl9.

Distinct in their green uniforms, the 95th Rifles are always popular at re-enactments and the recent success of the Sharpe television series has created much interest in these 'specialists'. Contact Les Handscombe, 48 Mutton Place, Prince Of Wales Road, London NWl 8DF (Tel: 0171 485 4942).

The Hoch und Deutschmeister are Britain's only Napoleonic Austrian regiment standing out at re-enactment events in their white uniforms. The unit has been in existence for over 20 years and has also forged strong links with other groups in Europe. Contact Ian Castle, 49 Belsize Park, London NW3 4EE.

La Garde Imperiale dedicates itself to recreating the glories of Napoleon's elite fighting force. The unit is particulary impressive because of its live firing displays using full size cannon, at the annual Euro Militaire model show at Folkestone and other events. Because of its reputation, the Garde has taken part in many prestigious events in France and from a foot and artillery group it has now diversified into cavalry, recruiting a group of Garde lancers. Members pay for their uniforms with a subscription of £20 per month. In the north, prospective recruits should contact Derek Mellard on 01924 381 820, Midlands, Jim Jackson, 01455 449 264, South, Jerry Lavender 01323 724 433.

The 9eme Demi-Brigade Legere dedicates itself to re-enacting the life and traditions of French soldiers during the revolutionary and Napoleonic periods and has become a particularly large unit, counting over 100 chasseurs in its ranks. Members pay £10 per month, which covers the cost of their uniforms and travel throughout Britain and Europe. Prospective recruits should be a minimum age of 15 and hold a current passport. Contact 'Louis' at 11 Birchwood Avenue, Wallington, Surrey, SM6 7HE (Tel: 0181 669 0900).

The 21eme Regiment De Ligne is another large re-enactment group with a membership of over 100 that always looks impressive at battle displays and living history events. The unit includes sappers, two eagle guards and an eagle bearer. Contact Chris Durkin 22 Swallow Street, Oldham, Lancashire OL8 4LD (Tel: 0161 652 1647).

France has an impressive range of re-enactment and study groups, particularly when it comes to the cavalry. One of the best groups is Les Hussards De Lasalle, 7 impasse des Balmes, 78450 Villepreux. Contact Jean Pierre Mir Del Rieu (Tel:(l) 30 56 24 16). Another fine group is Le lOe Escadron de Chasseurs à cheval de la garde 48, rue Chapon 75003 Paris. Contact Michel Pourrey (Tel: (1) 48 87 49 54).

The United States has seen the development of Napoleonic re-enacting in recent years. One of the biggest organisations is the Brigade Napoleon which has a number of good units and publishes the quarterly magazine *Le Ban*. Further details about the organisation are available from Brigade Napoleon, 18914 Walnut Road, Castro Valley, California 94546.

Canadian living history groups of the Napoleonic period: The 1st Regiment of Foot (Royal Scots), Light Company, to the period of the campaigns on the Niagara Frontier in 1813-1814, recreated by a large group based in the London (Ontario) area. For more information, contact: Steve Hartwick, 1543 Perth Avenue, London, ON, N5V 2M6, (519) 457-3832.

The Canadian Regiment of Fencible Infantry, Light company, to the War of 1812 period. This Canadian regular colonial unit is recreated in Eastern Ontario. For more information, contact: Mike Viger, #30-1491 Richmond Road, Ottawa, ON, K2B 6R9.

The Voltigeurs Canadiens/Canadian Voltigeurs, a regular colonial light infantry unit from Lower Canada (Quebec) which served in the War of 1812, recreated in Western Quebec and Eastern Ontario wearing its distinctive grey, trimmed black uniform. For more information, contact: Richard Beaudin, 6427 Timothy Crescent, Orleans, ON, K1C 3E5, (613) 824-9253. Fax (613) 837-8896.

Napoleonic re-enactment suppliers

Ages of Elegance at 480 Chiswick High Road London W4 5TT (Tel: 0181 742 0730) is run by Dawn Wood, an experienced re-enactor and costume expert whose clients include English Heritage, the 12th Light Dragoons and the Coldstream Guards Museum. Ages of Elegance accepts commissions to make uniforms and they also carry a range of buttons, leatherwork and other items in their shop which is a treasure trove for re-enactors.

The Plumery at 16 Deans Close, Whitehall Gardens, Chiswick London W4 3LX (Tel: 0181 995 7099) offers a wide selection of Napoleonic shakos from £85 and other headgear accoutrements. The plumery makes plumes for the British army, and with such exacting standards quality is assured.

Napoleonic Associations

With the success of the Sharpe television series, a fan club has been set up for Sharpe enthusiasts. The club has the approval of Richard Moore who is a consultant on the series and provides plenty of information. For further details contact Chris Clarke, East Lea, Brookfield Drive, Hoveringham, Notts, NG14 7JW.

The German States Study Group has been set up in the Napoleonic Association to study the period of German military history during the revolutionary and Napoleonic wars and sends out newsletters four times a year. For further information write to the Co-ordinator, John Henderson, 118 Milton Road, Hartlepool, Cleveland.

Though not exclusively Napoleonic, *La Sabretache*, France's long established society and magazine for military historians and collectors has published many excellent articles on Napoleonic uniforms. The *Bulletin de la Société des collectionneurs de figurines Historiques*, merged with the *La Sabretache* in the1970s and many great artists such as Lucien Rousselot and Eugene Leliepvre have been featured ln the journal. For further information write to *La Sabretache* 7 Rue Guersant, Paris 75017.

The Napoleonic Society of America is well worth joining for all Napoleonic enthusiasts. Membership includes a 40 page members' *Bulletin* with reports on Napoleonic sites and re-enactments and a conference is held every year. For further details write to the Napoleonic Society of America 5744 W. Irving Park Road, Chicago, Il, 60634.

Another leading society studying the life and times of Napoleon is the International Napoleonic Society. Details about the International Napoleonic Society are available from Ben Weider at 2875 Chemin Bates Road, Montreal, Quebec, Canada H35 IB7.

The Polish Military Collectors Association takes a strong interest in Poland's role in the Napoleonic Wars. The $50 annual dues include the society's magazine, *Hetman*. Further details from 168 Jackson Mill Road, Freehold NJ 07728, USA.

Museums with Napoleonic collections

The mecca for all Napoleonic enthusiasts is the Musée de L'Armée, Hotel National des Invalides, Paris. A staggering variety of Napoleonic uniforms are on display and the walls are festooned with pictures, many of them by the great French artist Édouard Détaille. Situated close to Napoleon's tomb, the museum offers plenty of material for even the most insatiable Napoleonic fan.

The Musée de L'Emperi at Château de L'Emperi Salon-de Provence 13300, is another fine museum featuring an outstanding collections of Napoleonic and Second Empire uniforms painstakingly built up in the Brunon Collection and now owned by the Musée de L'Armée.

Caillou, Napoleon's headquarters at Waterloo has been turned into a museum and you can see the rooms where Napoleon spent a fitful night before the battle and where he had breakfast on the morning of June 18 1815. A selection of battle flags is also on display.

The National Army Museum, Royal Hospital Road, Chelsea, London SW3 4HT, features The Road To Waterloo gallery telling the story of the Napoleonic Wars and incorporating a fine display of original artefacts including a captured French eagle and the hat General Picton was wearing when he was mortally wounded.

The Guards Museum at Wellington Barracks, Birdcage Walk, London SW41A 2AX has good displays on the Guards' Napoleonic service with special emphasis on their legendary defence of Hougoumont and their part in thwarting the attack of the Garde Imperiale at Waterloo.

The Museum of Artillery in the Rotunda, Woolwich, London SE18 4DN has much to offer the Napoleonic enthusiast. Displays include a six pounder cannon used by the Royal Horse Artillery in the Peninsula.

Near to the Museum of Artillery is the Royal Artillery Regimental Museum at the Old Royal Military Academy, Red Lion Lane, London SE18 4DN. In this museum the accent is more on uniforms, campaigns and equipment and a trip to both the Museum of Artillery and the Royal Artillery Regimental Museum, offers an ideal day out.

The Royal Regiment of Fusiliers Museum is situated in the Tower of London and again offers a worthwhile day out in conjunction with a visit to the Tower itself.

For a taste of the Duke of Wellington's life and times, a trip to his London residence at Apsley House, 149 Piccadilly, is a must. The house has been recently re-furbished and features a breathtaking display of Napoleonic memorabilia collected by and awarded to the Iron Duke.

Stratfield Saye House, near Reading in Berkshire, is the country residence of the Wellington family and also has many personal possessions of the first Duke. Also on display, is the first Duke's funeral hearse, made out of metal cast from melted down French cannon captured at Waterloo.

The Royal Green Jackets Museum, Peninsular Barracks, Romsey Road, Winchester, S023 8TS has exhibits on the role of riflemen in the Napoleonic Wars and also features a massive diorama of the Battle of Waterloo, which has over 20,000 figures and incorporates a sound and light commentary.

The Museum of The Duke of Edinburgh's Royal Regiment - Redcoats in The Wardrobe, 58 The Close, Salisbury, Wiltshire, SPl 2EX has exhibits on the 49th, 62nd and 66th Foot and is housed in a particularly elegant looking building.

Although a comparatively small unit in the Napoleonic Wars, the Royal Marines rendered good service and their story is told at the Royal Marines Museum, Southsea, Portsmouth, Hampshire, P04 9PX.

The achievements of the 3rd Foot, The Buffs, one of Britain's oldest regiments who saw many fine moments during the Napoleonic Wars is celebrated in the Buffs Regimental Museum at the Royal Museum, 18 High Street, Canterbury, Kent, CTl 2JE.

At Dover Castle in Kent you can see the additional towers added during the Napoleonic Wars and the inner bailey houses The Princess of Wales' Royal Regiment and Queen's Regiment Museum.

The Military Museum of Devon and Dorset situated in the Keep, Bridport Road, Dorchester, has a good selection of Napoleonic artefacts and some fine period paintings.

The Durham Light Infantry Museum, Aykley Heads, Durham City, has exhibits on the famed 68th Foot and their heroic actions in Wellington's Peninsular campaigns. The colours of the regiment are laid up in nearby Durham Cathedral.

The Duke of Wellington's Regimental Museum at the Bankfield Museum Akroyd Park, Halifax, traces the services of the 33rd Foot and 76th Foot and also has some artefacts connected with Wellington himself.

The Worcestershire Regimental Museum at Worcester City Museum, Foregate Street, Worcester, mainly concentrates on the history of the 29th and 36th Foot. The Worcesters stood firm at Rolica in

1808 and 'Firm' became their regimental motto.

Artefacts of the Royal Scots Dragoon Guards, the heroic Greys, whose charge at Waterloo is one of the best known aspects of the battle, are housed at Edinburgh Castle and the Scottish United Services Museum in the Castle has many items of interest to Napoleonic enthusiasts.

The Black Watch Museum at Balhousie Castle, Perth, commemorates the famous 42nd Foot who fought gallantly at Quatre-Bras. The museum also has exhibits on the 73rd Foot.

The Regimental Museum of the Royal Welch Fusiliers in the Queen's Tower, Caernarfon Castle, Caernarfon, Gwynedd, has some particularly interesting material on the regiment's servive during the Peninsular campaign.

The Regimental Museum of the Queen's Dragoon Guards at Cardiff Castle, has a fine uniform collection including items worn at Waterloo.

Napoleonic Book Suppliers

One of the most popular periods of military history, a vast selection of books on the Napoleonic period is available both new and secondhand. The following is a list of some of the leading suppliers.

Caliver Books, 816-818 London Road, Leigh-on-Sea Essex SS9 3NH, (Tel & Fax 01702 73986), offer a big selection of Napoleonic Books from uniform studies to a selection of Bernard Cornwell's Sharpe novels.

Hersant's Military Books, whose shop on the Archway Road in North London was a favourite haunt for book enthusiasts, now operate a mail order service from 17 The Drive. High Barnet, Hertfordshire, EN5 4JG (Tel: 0181- 440- 6816, Fax: 0181 440-6816) and have a good selection of Napoleonic books.

Francis Edwards the long experienced military history booksellers who were established in 1855 and have their shop at 13 Great Newport Street, Charing Cross Road, London WC2H 7JA, (Tel: 0171-379-7699 Fax: 0171-836-5977) offer a range of secondhand Napoleonic books for collectors on big and small budgets.

Ken Trotman Ltd, Unit 11, 135 Ditton Walk, Cambridge, CB5 8PY (Tel: 01223 211030. Fax: 01223 212317), issues three free catalogues a year, featuring a good Napoleonic selection.

Victor Sutcliffe, 36 Parklands Road, London SW16 6TE (Tel: 0181-769-8345. Fax: 0181-769 6446) is a specialist in the Napoleonic era and issues a Napoleonic book catalogue. His premises are open by appointment.

Chelifer Books at Todd Close, Curthwaite,

Wigton, Cumbria CA7 8BE (Tel & Fax 01228 711388) offers a choice selection of Napoleonic books. Wanted lists are accepted, visitors by appointment.

Worley Publications & Booksellers, 10 Rectory Road East, Felling, Tyne and Wear NE10 9DN (Tel: 0191 469 2414), offer a range of facsimile reprints including *The Recollections of Colonel de Gonneville* who rose through the ranks of the French army to become a major in the 13th Cuirassiers.

Napoleonic Art

Cranston Fine Arts, Torwood House, Torwoodhill Road, Rhu, Helensburgh, G84 8LE (Tel: 01436 820 269) are the agents for widely acclaimed Napoleonic artist Mark Churms and also offer a range of prints of classic paintings by other artists including Caton Woodville's *Defiant Highlander* and *Wellington At Waterloo* by Crofts. In the United States and Canada, Cranston are represented by Fredericksburg Historical Prints, 829 Caroline Street, Fredericksburg, VA 22401 (Tel: 540 373 1861) and the Military Art Gallery, 19358 Kelly Road, Harper Woods, MI 48225 (Tel: 313 6521 6420).

American artist Keith Rocco is the United States' leading exponent of painting the Napoleonic period and he's also renowned for his work on the American Civil War. Rocco's recent works include the Lincolnshires in action at Waterloo and portrait pieces of a French Grenadier officer and a Cuiraissier officer. One of the main outlets for limited edition prints of Rocco's work is the Tradition Studio, PO Box 779, Woodstock, VA 22644 (Tel: 540 459 5469 or 540 459 5951).

Ed Dovey whose work has been extensively featured in *Military Illustrated* and other magazines and books offers some of his orginal artwork for sale. write to Ed at 70 Clement Close, Willesden, London NW8 7AN.

Bob Cowan, 100 Kiowa Drive South, Lake Kiowa, TX 76240 USA. (Tel: 817-668-6420) offer slides and prints of the famous Knötel range of plates of Napoleonic uniforms.

Pompadour Gallery, P.O. Box II, Romford, Essex RM7 7HY has Napoleonic subjects in their vast range of military postcards.

Le Cimier, 38 Rue Ginoux, 75015, Paris, feature plates of Napoleonic subjects by leading French artist Pierre Conrad, whose work is full of vigour and very exacting.

The Red Lancer Inc, PO Box 8050, Mesa, AZ 85214 USA (Tel: 602 964 9667. Fax: 602 890 9495) offers Napoleonic prints and fine art, rare books, military artefacts and medals. Catalogues printed four or five times a year, are available by subscription and cost $12 dollars for America, $20 for Canada and $35 for overseas.

Napoleonic Model Soldiers and Wargame Figures

Sculptor Maurice Corry produces 120mm resin and white metal Napoleonic models available through his company The Roll Call, 316 Goodyers End Lane, Bedworth, Warwickshire CV12 OHY (Tel or Fax 01203 494123). Releases include a Chasseur à cheval of the Imperial Guard, and an ensign of the 1st Foot, Royal Scots, at Waterloo carrying the regimental colours.

David Grieve runs D.F. Grieve Models, St Andrews, Westwood Road, Betsham Nr Gravesend, Kent DA13 9LZ. His work includes a selection of 100mm figures of the British army at Waterloo; and the range includes an officer of the Royal Horse Artillery, and a sergeant of the 79th Cameron Highlanders.

Poste Militaire feature a range of definitive Napoleonic miniatures in their range of figures, including magnificent 90mm mounted models of a French hussar trumpeter and a trooper of the 2nd Regiment red lancers. Poste Militaire are at Station Road, Northiam, Rye, East Sussex TN31 6QT,

Metal Modeles, the French firm run by talented sculptor Bruno Leibovitz, produces some exquiste French Napoleonic subjects in 54mm including a mounted dragoon and a range of French light infantry. Leibovitz has also sculpted a magnificent large scale French hussar. Metal Modeles are at BP 66, La Queniere, Route de Mons, 83440 Fayence.

Among the range of figures produced by Le Cimier, 38 Rue Ginoux, 75015, Paris, are a range of busts of Napoleonic French army soldiers. The range includes a hussar and a carabinier.

Tradition of London Ltd at 33 Curzon Street, Mayfair, London, W1Y 7AE (Tel: 0171 493 7452, Fax: 0171 355 1224) and Under Two Flags, 4 St Christopher's Place, Oxford Street, London W1 (Tel or fax 0171 935 6934) both stock a variety of Napoleonic figures. One of Tradition's latest releases is a set of toy figures depicting some of the characters in the Sharpe series.

Napoleonic figures are continuing to grow in the range produced by the Italian company, Pegaso. The list includes a magnificent 90mm hussar of the Neapolitan Guard 1812-1815, sculpted by Luca Marchetti. Pegaso Models are at C.P., 99 Siena Centro, 53100 Siena, Italy.

Relocated to America from Belgium, Verlinden Productions at the VLS Corporation, 811 Lone Star Drive. O'Fallon, Missouri 63366 are producing some 120mm resin Napoleonic figures including an officer of the Polish lancers of the Imperial Guard, a French hussar officer and a figure of the flamboyant French cavalry commander, Lasalle.

Fort Duquesne miniatures, 105 Tristan Drive, Pittsburgh PA 15209, USA have a 120mm mounted French cuirassier, 1812, in their range sculpted by Mike Tapavica. A bust of a 95th Rifleman, sculpted by rising British talent Jon Cheeseman.

Many of the figures mentioned above and other Napoleonic miniatures are stocked by Historex Agents, Wellington House, 157 Snargate Street, Dover, Kent, CT17 9BZ. One of the largest model mail order specialists in the world, Historex Agents also stock the legendary 54mm Historex plastic kits that revolutionised the model soldier hobby back in the 70s and which are still very popular today.

British, French, Russian, Prussian and Austrian 25mm wargame figures are part of the vast Napoleonic range produced by Connoisseur Figures at 27 Sandycombe Road, Kew, Richmond, Surrey TW9 2EP (Phone & Fax 0181 940 8156).

Bicorne Miniatures have a range of 25mm Napoleonic miniatures and £1 will bring you a price list and a sample figure. Write to Brian Holland, 40 Churrch Road, Uppermill, Oldham, OL3 6EL.

Irregular Miniatures of 69A Acomb Road, Holgate, York, Y02 4EP (Tel: 01904 790 597) have brought out a range of 42mm Napoleonic figures for the wargamer and collector. The range includes French line infantry and British light infantry.

Minifigs, one of the originators of wargame figures, are still producing a wide range of Napoleonic figures. For details write to Minifigs at 1-5 Graham Road, Southampton S014 OAX.

Elite Miniatures of 26 Bowlease Gardens, Bessacarr, Doncaster, South Yorkshire, DN4 6AP (Tel: 01302 530038) produce high quality 25mm Napoleonic figures for the wargamer and collector including a particularly fine Peninsular Campaign British foot artillery battery.

Wargames Foundry of the Foundry, Mount Street, New Basford, Nottingham, NG7 7HX produce quality 25mm ranges of Napoleonic figures from 1805-1815 and also from the French Revolutionary Wars 1789-1802.

Dixon Miniatures at Spring Grove Mills, Linthwaite, Huddersfield, West Yorkshire, HD7 5QG (Tel and fax: 01484 646 162) include an extensive range of 25mm Napoleonic figures in their range of wargaming figures.

Index

Acknowledgements

The author would like to thank the
following people and organisations without
whose help this study would have been
impossible: Francis Back, Montreal; Raoul
Brunon of the Musée de l'Armée, Salon-de-
Provence; Col. John R. Elting, Cornwall,
New York; Adrian Forman, Minehead,
Somerset; Peter Harrington of the Anne
S.K. Brown Military Collection, Brown
University, Providence, Rhode Island; Don
Troiani, Southbury, Connecticut; Tim
Newark of Military Illustrated, London;
Col. Jacques Ostiguy, Ottawa, Ontario;
Michel Pétard, Nantes, France; Robin
Smith regarding the Directory. And, last
but not least, my wife Luce and my two
sons Louis and Alexandre for their patience
and support.